Easy Peasy Language Arts 6 Lesson Guide

Cover Design: Stephen Rutherford

Welcome to the EP Language Arts 6 Lesson Guide!

This book teaches the lessons you'll need to complete the Language Arts 6 Workbook. It was written for the student. You should read the lesson each lesson and then follow the directions on the worksheet for that lesson in your workbook.

The answers for the workbook are in the back of this book. Complete your worksheet before checking your answers. Learn from your mistakes. Mistakes are learning opportunities. Don't waste your opportunities! If you cheat and just copy answers, you are only cheating yourself. The point is to learn and to educate yourself. Education is power. Cheating is lazy. Lazy people aren't powerful!

This course covers all language arts topics including: writing, grammar, and spelling. Throughout the year students will be writing non-fiction essays, and the year ends with writing a research report. You will practice creative, descriptive writing as well.

If you get to the end of a page, turn the page to see if there is more to your lesson!

Have a great year!

Note: We used to call each lesson a day: "Day 1," "Day 2," etc. We've replaced those days with "lessons," but you'll see "day" still in the mini pages in the answer section. Those pages are the same, not outdated, just that one word is changed.

Lesson 1
1. I write lots of directions, not just in this course, but in all of them. I want you to be careful to read them all before you start working. It's always important to read the directions. It could save you work! Sometimes, especially in math, I will tell you to only answer the even numbered questions or to only do a certain number of rows, but you could go and answer them all if you didn't read the directions first!
2. So, today's assignment is to practice following directions. You can find your directions in your workbook. Use the page labeled for Lesson 1. Every day you'll complete the workbook page with the corresponding lesson number, unless I let you know there is no workbook page for that lesson.

Lesson 2
1. I hope you followed all the directions carefully in lesson 1 and ended up writing only your name on the page.
2. You are going to be editing sentences today. Here's what to look for:
    - Spelling
    - Capitalization
        - Proper nouns: meaning names of places, names of people, names of things
        - First word in each sentence
    - Punctuation
        - Sentences end with punctuation.
        - Apostrophes show contractions and possession. It's Mike's bike.
        - Commas separate date words and numbers, items in a list, introductory words from the rest of the sentence, and parts of a compound sentence.
            - A comma and then conjunction separate the parts of a compound sentences.
3. You need to find a partner to check your guesses to play the hangman game on the workbook page for today. They can find the words on the answer page for Lesson 2 in the back of this book.

Lesson 3
1. A syllable is a word part. Saying a word in its syllables can help you spell and read it. Clapping while you say a word can help you determine the number of syllables, but my favorite method is to place your hand under your chin. Every time your chin goes down, that's a syllable.
2. Try it with these words: straw, bucket, terrible, unbelievable
    - They have 1, 2, 3, and 5 syllables respectively. Is that what you got? When you are ready, you can try the syllable part of your worksheet for Lesson 3.
3. You again need a helper to complete today's lesson. Find someone to read you the words on the answer page for Lesson 3. Afterwards, check your answers and fix your mistakes or rewrite any missed words the correct way to help it get in your brain.

Lesson 4

1. On your worksheet you are going to be editing again today like in lesson 2. Take a peek back at Lesson 2 above for a reminder of some grammar rules.
   - One new punctuation mark to mention is the hyphen. It's used in the spelling of some words, like numbers, and to connect adjectives that work together to describe a noun. We'll learn more about using hyphens in adjectives later in the year.
2. To practice your spelling some more, complete the word search.

Lesson 5

1. Write a poem in the same form as this one. More directions follow.

   Two roads diverged in a yellow wood,
   And sorry I could not travel both
   And be one traveler, long I stood
   And looked down one as far as I could
   To where it bent in the undergrowth;

2. It is written in the form: ABAAB. These letters show that each stanza has five lines.
3. The matching letters show which lines rhyme. In this poem the "B lines" rhyme, the second and last lines, and the "A lines" rhyme, the first, third, and fourth lines.
4. Also pay attention to the length of each line. Each line in the first stanza is nine syllables long. (A stanza is what we call each paragraph of a poem or song.)
5. On your worksheet, you will write one stanza, trying to make each of the five lines nine syllables long and using the rhyme scheme, ABAAB.

Lesson 6

1. You have a longer story for editing today on your worksheet in your workbook.
2. Peek back at Lesson 2 if you want a review. I'll give you a hint; you'll need to be on the lookout for commas after introductory phrases. They are dependent clauses, parts of the sentence that don't stand alone.

Lesson 7

1. Write a short story in your workbook today.
2. Get a high five and/or hug for every vocabulary word from your reading assignments that you put into your story.

Lesson 8

1. You are going to be identifying parts of speech in your workbook today.
2. Here's a reminder.
   - Noun: person, place, or thing (Riding my bike is fun. Riding my bike is the "thing" the sentence is about. Riding is a noun in that sentence. I go for a morning walk. Walk is a thing in that sentence.)
   - Verb: action or state of being (is, am, are)
   - Adjective: describes nouns
   - Adverb: describes adjectives, adverbs, or verbs
   - Preposition: location word that always has an object (on the bed, under my foot, into the house, with me, around here)

Lesson 9

1. You are going to be identifying parts of speech in your workbook again today.
2. This time you are given the part of speech, and you need to find the word.

Lesson 10

1. Today you are going to practice writing better sentences. Combine the sentences into one long sentence.
2. Here's an example for you.
   - I have four brothers.
   - One has two dogs that he brings to family gatherings.
   - They all come home for Thanksgiving.
   - They each have their own family.
     - Even though each of my four brothers has their own family now, they all come home for Thanksgiving, one even bringing his two dogs along.
     - P.S. This is totally made up. I have one brother. It's just an example.
3. There are no right and wrong answers for this. You can see I didn't use everything in the sentences. You can adapt the sentences to fit them together.
4. When you are done, you can check the examples in the answers for a comparison.

Lesson 11

1. Do today's worksheet on metaphors.
2. It is a reminder of something that you hopefully know, that a metaphor is a description where one thing is said to be something else.

Lesson 12

1. Write three metaphors on your worksheet. Get a high five and/or hug if you use one of your vocabulary words (from another course).
2. Here's an example of one: The fog horn was a baritone making his presence known with a low operatic note.

Lesson 13

1. Unscramble the words on your worksheet today to practice spelling.
2. They all begin with the letter E.

Lesson 14

1. Fix the sentences on your worksheet. They are all fragments, incomplete sentences. Make them into proper sentences.
   - Sentences need a subject and a predicate, the thing the sentence is about and what about it. That means that every sentence must have a noun and a verb.
   - There are rare cases when the subject is just understood. Like your mother saying, "Go clean your room." You understand that you are the subject of the sentence.
2. The second part of the page deals with correct word choice.
   - I is the subject pronoun and me is the object pronoun. You have to decide if it's being used as part of the subject or not.
   - Use the sentences following to make sure you're thinking straight about these often confused words.

- They're over there fixing their wagon.
- It's too hot for the two of you to run around so much.

Lesson 15
1. On your worksheet today, you'll be identifying similes. They are similar to metaphors in that they are comparing two unlike things. The difference is that they use the words like or as to do it.
   - You're an ice cube. (metaphor)
   - You're as cold as ice. (simile)
2. When you are done, you'll write a simile that includes an animal.

Lesson 16
1. Write about a time when either you treated someone differently because of how they looked or you treated someone the same despite how they looked.
2. If you can't think of a time, what about a time when you were treated differently because of how you looked?

Lesson 17
1. Write a simile about yourself.
2. Write a metaphor about yourself.

Lesson 18
1. On your worksheet, write the verb that correctly completes the sentence. You will be using the present tense. The <u>present tense</u> talks about something that <u>happens</u> now, not about something that *happened* in the past or that *will happen* in the future.
   - I underlined the present tense of to happen. The italicized words are to happen in the past and future tenses.
2. Be careful to find the subject and to match the verb to it.
   - A singular subject needs a singular verb.
   - He has (singular).
   - They have (plural).

Lesson 19
1. You are going to need help with this one. Grab someone to read the story from the answer key.
2. Spell the words into the blanks as they read.
3. Correct any of your mistakes. Learn the correct spelling of any you get wrong.

Lesson 20
1. Do the simile exercise in your workbook. You are creating the similes that make the most sense.
2. They are common similes, so maybe you recognize most of them. You'll want to try to make up new and interesting similes in your writing.

Lesson 21
1. Read this poem by Jacqueline Sweeny.
   - *Edible*
     My shirt is red tomato soup,
     My pockets are green peas.
     My khakis are brown dog biscuits.
     My socks are cottage cheese.
     I have vanilla ice-cream shoes
     with limp spaghetti bows.
     I wish I could eat everything,
     but then I'd have no clothes!
2. Choose a noun. Choose two adjectives that describe that noun. Turn each into a metaphor.
3. EXAMPLE… apple; red, delicious
   - My apple is red becomes my apple has blushing cheeks.
   - My apple is delicious becomes my apple is a symphony in my mouth.

Lesson 22
1. Do it again.
2. Choose a noun. Choose two adjectives that describe that noun. Turn each into a metaphor.
3. EXAMPLE… apple; red, delicious
   - My apple is red becomes my apple has blushing cheeks.
   - My apple is delicious becomes my apple is a symphony in my mouth.

Lesson 23
1. Proofread the sentences on your worksheet today. You need to make sure you create complete sentences.
2. Every sentence needs a subject and a verb and can't be combined with another sentence without punctuation.
3. Introductory phrases are followed by a comma and need the independent clause following. Introductory phrases aren't complete sentences on their own.

Lesson 24
1. Proofread the sentences in your workbook today. This is just like Lesson 23's assignment.
2. If you aren't sure about one, just read it out loud. That will help you hear if it's a complete sentence or not.

Lesson 25
1. You are editing today, looking for word choice, spelling, and punctuation mistakes.
   - Here's something that will help you. Further and farther both describe going on, but <u>farther</u> refers to distance. You can remember that because how <u>far</u> something is tells its distance.
2. There is a second part on your worksheet. You are going to be writing the plural spelling of the words.

- Words that end in X, S, CH, SH are followed by an ES when made plural.
- You can hear the difference.
  - bikes (one syllable)
  - peaches (two syllables – You say the ES.)
3. If a word ends in a consonant and then an O, you *often* add an ES as well.
   - tomatoes, but videos
   - heroes, but pianos
4. When a word ends with the F or FE, it changes into a V and ends with ES.
   - wolf : wolves
   - wife : wives

Lesson 26
1. You are editing again today on your worksheet. When it says five spelling mistakes, the same word spelled incorrectly more than once counts as more than one spelling mistake.
   - You'll be looking for similar things as before, such as commas before conjunctions to separate two independent sentences and commas to separate out introductory or unnecessary information, things that could be taken out and you'd still be left with a full sentence.
2. On the bottom of the page is plurals. Peek up at Lesson 25 for some rule reminders. Here are some more by example.
   - vertebra : vertebrae
   - bacterium : bacteria
   - cactus : cacti (octopus : octopuses is an exception)
   - vertex : vertices (complex : complexes is an exception)
   - crisis : crises (pronounced : cry – sees)

Lesson 27
1. Write about an imaginary country in your workbook today. It needs a name, a language, and a currency.
2. It also needs a national identity. What makes it unique? What is its character?

Lesson 28
1. You'll need help for this one.
2. Nicely ask someone to read you the words in the answer key for Lesson 28.
3. Rewrite any word you spell incorrectly to practice writing it the correct way.

Lesson 29
1. Go through this dialogue lesson before you complete your dialogue worksheet page where you'll write examples. This is in preparation for a dialogue you will be writing in lesson 30.
2. Dialogue is a conversation and an important part of writing novels. Read these two dialogues.

Mary: Hello, Tom. How are you today?
Tom: Hello, Mary. I am fine today. Who is your friend with you?
Mary: This is Susan.

Susan: I am Mary's new neighbor. I am going to begin going to school here.
Tom: It is nice to meet you, Susan. Welcome to our school.
Susan: Thank you, Tom, for welcoming me.

Mary: Hey, Tom. What's up?
Tom: Nothing. Who's this?
Mary: This is…
Susan: I'm Susan. I'm her new neighbor. I'm starting school here.
Tom: Nice to meet you. Welcome.
Susan: Thanks.

- What is the difference?
- Why doesn't the first sound real? What's changed in the second one?
  - There is the use of pronouns, informal speech, contractions, incomplete sentences, speaker is cut off…
3. Dialogue isn't supposed to be proper writing. It's supposed to sound like you speaking.
4. This next dialogue is written as if it were in a book.

Hey!" called Mary to get Tom's attention. "What's up?"
"Nothing. Who's this?"
"This is…" Mary started her introduction, but the new girl jumped in.
"I'm Susan." She was almost as tall as Tom and looked right into his eyes.
"I'm her new neighbor. I'm starting school here."
"Nice to meet you," he said with a smile, "and welcome."
"Thanks." Susan returned the grin.

5. As long as you know who is speaking. You don't need —he said, —she said which are called **speech tags**. You can use **action tags** which tell what the person is doing or **descriptive tags** which describe something about that person in order to show who is talking. You can see examples of this in the dialogue, lines 4 and 6 (labeled at the end of part six of this assignment).
6. Here are some grammar rules for writing dialogue. In ( ) you will see what lines are examples of this rule.
   - Each new speaker starts a new paragraph. (1-6)
   - Commas, periods, etc. go inside of the quotation marks. (1-6)
   - Quotation marks enclose everything that is being said. (1-6)
   - Quotation marks can close and then open again in the middle of a sentence. (5)
   - Commas end most quotations if they are followed by a speech tag. (5)
   - Periods instead of commas should be used if the tag is not a speech tag. (4, 6)
   - You can use an exclamation point or question mark instead of a comma. (1)
   - The punctuation goes inside the quotation marks. (5-6)
   - A speech tag starts with a lowercase letter unless it is a proper noun. (1, 6)
   - Make sure it is clear who is speaking. Be sure to describe how they are saying things (shyly, snidely) and what the characters are doing (smiling, hanging their head).

1"Hey!" called Mary to get Tom's attention. "What's up?"
1. "Nothing. Who's this?"
2. "This is…" Mary started her introduction, but the new girl jumped in.
3. "I'm Susan." She was almost as tall as Tom and looked right into his eyes. "I'm her new neighbor. I'm starting school here."
4. "Nice to meet you," he said with a smile, "and welcome."
5. "Thanks." Susan returned the grin.
7. Write an example of dialogue that uses each a speech tag, a descriptive tag, and an action tag.

Lesson 30
1. Choose any character from a book you are reading and write a dialogue between you and the character. Use your workbook page for today.
2. Use the directions above to remember your grammar rules for writing dialogue.

Lesson 31
1. Here are the rules of commas.
   - Use a comma when separating **items in a series**. Some people drop the comma before the last and, but it is not wrong to use it, and sometimes wrong to not use it, so I say always put a comma before the last item in a series.
     - We stopped at the store, the gas station, and the post office.
   - Use a comma between **interchangeable adjectives**, when you could put "and" between them.
     - You can say the feeble, old man or the old, feeble man.
       - the feeble and old man – the old and feeble man
     - You most naturally say the three adorable puppies, not the adorable three puppies.
       - The three and adorable puppies? No.
   - Don't use a comma where a semicolon or period should go. It's a run-on sentence called a **comma splice**.
     - Go home quickly, mom needs you. WRONG
     - Go home quickly. Mom needs you.
   - **When two independent clauses are joined with a conjunction**, then you do use a comma before the conjunction.
     - I need to go, but I am not ready yet.
   - If more than one verb is used with a subject, then a comma is not generally used before the second verb. In general, **you never put one comma between a subject and verb**.
     - He packed up his things and left the house.
   - A comma **follows an introductory dependent clause**, one that can't stand alone.
     - If I do this, you better be there to help me out.
     - When I get home, we'll practice.
       - A comma isn't needed if the parts of the sentence are reversed.
         - We'll practice when I get home.

- Sometimes the comma after introductory phrases, especially very short ones is optional. However, there are many **words and short phrases that introduce** a sentence alone that are followed by a comma.
  - After dinner we'll play a game.
  - Yes, I believe so.
  - For instance, this will do.
- Always use a comma where it is needed to **make the meaning clear**.
  - Monday night football was cancelled. Monday night, football was cancelled.
    - Was football cancelled Monday night, or is football played Monday nights cancelled for good?
- Commas separate out appositives, **extra info that is unnecessary** to the sentences.
  - Jill, who is loving her job, is in charge of check-in.
  - The key is unnecessary information. If it's needed to identify what you are talking about, then it is necessary.
- Commas surround **words that interrupt** a sentence.
  - I came here today, as you know, on a very important mission.
- Commas **surround names when the person is being addressed**, even if they are titles or nicknames or terms of endearment.
  - Honey, could you help me with this?
  - Thank you, Mr. President.
  - Yes, Ella, I will.
- Commas **separate date words and numbers**. If a full date is in the middle of a sentence, a comma comes after the year as well.
  - The acceptance of the Declaration of Independence on July 2, 1776, was a turning point in history.
  - Monday, June 28th is an important day.
- Use a comma **before and after a state when used with its city**.
  - I have visited the historical sites in Philadelphia, Pennsylvania, many times.
    - Think of the state as an unnecessary description and that's why it is sectioned off.
- Use a comma **before and after an abbreviation at the end of a name or title**.
  - Jennifer Greene, Ph.D., is here as the speaker.
  - Dr. Rev. Martin Luther King, Jr., was an influential leader.
- Use a comma **before quotation marks when they are part of the same sentence**.
  - "Yes, sir," he answered, "I would like that."
  - Exception is when the words in quotes aren't being spoken.
    - "Whatever" is an overused term.
- Use a comma to **separate a statement and question and contrasting parts** of a sentence.
  - I believe him, don't you?
  - I have taste, but you don't.

2. On your worksheet today, you'll have to write sentences using some of these rules. Your worksheet will tell you which ones.

Lesson 32
1. In your opinion, which episode so far, in a book you are reading for school or one you've recently read for fun, has been the most entertaining? Why?
2. Make sure to use your workbook page to explain thoroughly. For instance, if you say because it is funny, then give three examples of funny things that happened.

Lesson 33
1. On your worksheet today you'll be identifying the sentence that uses commas correctly.
2. You can use the list in Lesson 31 to help you if you need the reminder.

Lesson 34
1. A simple sentence has one independent clause.
   - It can be a very long sentence with lots of words and still be a simple sentence.
2. A compound sentence is two independent clauses connected with a conjunction.
   - There is one sentence with a subject and predicate, and then there is another one with its own subject and verb clause that can stand on its own.
3. A complex sentence has a dependent clause and an independent clause.
   - When you are complex, part of your sentence has a noun and verb but can't stand on its own.
   - It relies on the rest of the sentence because it is dependent on it.
4. I hope you noticed that each bullet point is an example of the type of sentence.
5. Look for each type of sentence in a book. You'll copy them into your workbook for today.

Lesson 35
1. Choose a setting from a book, maybe one you are reading for school, and write about a day you spent there. Use simple, compound, and complex sentences.
2. Make sure this gets saved; you need this for Lesson 36's grammar lesson.

Lesson 36
1. Let's look again at simple, compound, and complex sentences.
   - A phrase is a group of words, one piece of information – the funny clown.
   - A clause is a group of words that contains a noun and verb – the funny clown was silly.
   - An independent clause can stand alone as a sentence.
     - The funny clown was silly.
   - A dependent clause cannot.
     - When the funny clown was silly
   - Simple and compound sentences are made with independent clauses.
   - Complex sentences have both independent and dependent clauses.
2. Try the activity in your workbook for today and check your answers. Once you understand all the correct answers, try the following activity.
3. Use your writing assignment from Lesson 35 and underline every sentence.

- Use three different colored pencils and color code your story.
- Every sentence should be underlined marking it as simple, compound, or complex.
- Assign a color to each type of sentence.

4. Make sure your comma usage is correct.

Lesson 37

1. Governments have often been accused of rewriting history. You try it for your writing assignment today in your workbook.
2. Choose a famous event in history and rewrite it. Was Benedict Arnold really the hero of the American Revolution? You decide.

Lesson 38

1. You'll be spelling in your workbook today.
2. You'll need someone to read the story to you from the answer key.

Lesson 39

1. Look at some ways to combine sentences.
   - My brother writes for magazines.
   - My brother is an avid outdoorsman.
     - My brother, a magazine writer, is an avid outdoorsman.
     - An avid outdoorsman, my brother writes for magazines.
     - My brother is a magazine writer and an avid outdoorsman.
     - Using his adventures as an avid outdoorsman, my brother writes for magazines.
     - My brother, writing for magazines, finds his inspiration by being an avid outdoorsman.
2. Write better sentences by combining the information on your worksheet today. Pay attention to commas!
3. Combine the sentences into one, and then check the answer key. They don't have to be identical but learn from the examples.

Lesson 40

1. On your worksheet for today you are going to try to find the common comma errors.
2. Lesson 31 has the long lesson on commas if you want to look back.

Lesson 41

1. There is a spelling activity on your worksheet today.
2. Make sure you write out any words you missed so that you practice them correctly.

Lesson 42

1. On your worksheet for today, try combining sentences again.
2. Are you better at it now? Don't forget those commas!

Lesson 43

1. Copy the best sentence from a chapter you read today or from a book you have recently read. It could be the most exciting, the most descriptive, the funniest, the cleverest…. Label it with the book title and page number.
2. What makes it so great? Write your answer on your workbook page under your sentence.
3. Now label the parts of speech in your sentence. Use colors, numbers, arrows, etc., whatever you choose, but make a key on the page to show your system.
4. What type of sentence is it? (ie. simple, compound, complex)

Lesson 44

1. Turn back to Lesson 36 and refresh your memory about clauses.
2. Try the independent clause activity in your workbook.

Lesson 45

1. Make a poster about a book you have recently read or are close to finishing.
   - If you are using the *EP Sixth Reader*, your poster should be on one of the themes you took notes on as you read *Gulliver's Travels*.
2. Include on your poster three examples from your book.
3. Include biographical information on the author.
4. Include a title for the poster and explanation of what your poster shows.
5. Present your poster.
   - It should be neat, organized, appealing, easy to read by your audience.
6. An alternative is to prepare a power point type of presentation including the same things.
7. Today you just have to plan it out. On your workbook page, gather quotes and examples from the book. The **deadline** is Lesson 50.

Lesson 46

1. Research the author. How does the author's background make him or her suited to writing this novel?
2. On your workbook page, record what you learn about the author. Decide what you want to include in the presentation.
3. Have you found the three examples that you want to include from the book?

Lesson 47

1. On your workbook page, write a short summary of your book.
2. You can use this at the beginning of your presentation. You could read it to your audience or create a final draft of it to include on your project.

Lesson 48

1. Put together your presentation.
2. Here's a reminder of your directions.
   - Make a poster about a book you have recently read or are close to finishing. Include on your poster three examples from your book.
   - Include any biographical information on the author.
   - Include a title for the poster and explanation of what your poster shows.
   - Present your poster.

- It should be neat, organized, appealing, easy to read by your audience.
3. An alternative is to prepare a power point type of presentation including the same things.

Lesson 49
1. Finish your presentation!
2. Do your best!

Lesson 50
1. Present your poster or power point.
   - Read your title.
   - Tell a little about the book.
   - Share about the author.
   - Share the examples from the book.
   - Answer any questions.
   - If you are using the EP Sixth Reader, explain the theme you chose and how the examples from the book show the theme.
2. Ask a parent to take a picture for your portfolio.

Lesson 51
1. There are two parts to your worksheet today. Go over the dialogue lesson below and try the activity in the workbook to practice punctuating dialogue.
2. Here are two different ways of punctuating dialogue from the book *The King Will Make a Way*.
   - The first example is the most common way.

   "Our spies tell us that in the morning Vulpine will condescend to be among the common folk," Stone mocked.

     - "Stone mocked" is a speech tag. This type of tag is preceded by a comma. If you were telling this to someone you would say, "Stone mocked that our spies…"
     - If you were telling someone a story, you wouldn't say, "It's number five. He said." You would say, "He said it was number five."
       - You can see how this type of tag is part of the sentence.
       - The comma (instead of a period) keeps it as part of the sentence.
     - By the way, if it was a question or exclamation, you would keep those punctuation marks.
       - "She said what?" she asked again.
       - Notice the lower case she…remember it's all part of the same sentence.
3. A second example:
   - "They are greedy for money and power and despise virtue." Stone rose and began methodically pacing the length of the room.
     - This quote is followed by an action tag. It's not a he said, she said tag. It's describing what the character did. This type of tag is preceded by a period, or question mark, or exclamation point. It is its own sentence.

- You could also tell who's speaking by using a description. This is also its own sentence and doesn't use the comma like a speech tag.
  - Rachel's eyes were shining. "I'll be there."
  - A speech tag would look like this: Rachel's eyes were shining as she said, "I'll be there."
4. Use the dialogue below to review these grammar rules.
  - Each new speaker starts a new paragraph. (1-6)
  - Commas, periods, etc. go inside of the quotation marks. (1-6)
  - Quotation marks enclose everything that is being said. (1-6)
  - Quotation marks can close and then open again in the middle of a sentence. (5)
  - Commas end most quotations if they are followed by a speech tag. (2, 5)
  - Periods instead of commas should be used if the tag is not a speech tag. (4, 6)
  - You can use an exclamation point or question mark instead of a comma. (1)
  - The punctuation goes inside the quotation marks. (1-6)
  - A speech tag starts with a lowercase letter unless it is a proper noun. (1, 5)

  1 – "Hey!" called Mary to get Charity's attention. "What's up?"
  2 - "Nothing," Charity answered. "Who's this?"
  3 - "This is—" Mary started to say, but the new girl jumped in.
  4 - "I'm Susan." She was taller than Charity and looked her in the eyes. "I'm her new neighbor. I'm starting school here."
  5 - "Nice to meet you," she said with a smile, "and welcome."
  6 - "Thanks." Susan returned the grin.

5. Then choose someone from history whom you have recently studied or that you find interesting. This is the start to a biographical essay you will be writing. Today, find an interesting quote by that person.
  - Onto your workbook page copy the quote as well as the title, author, and date written from where you got the quote.

Lesson 52
1. Cut out the squares from your worksheet for today. Rearrange them in different ways to make different dialogues.
2. You'll also need to collect ten facts about the person you chose in lesson 51. Write them on the other workbook page for today.
3. You will be writing a biographical essay. Today you are just collecting ten facts. I'll walk you through the essay step by step.
4. You'll be using the checklist in lesson 64 to help you correct it when you are done. You should take a look because you should be aiming to include all of those things as you write your essay.

Lesson 53
1. Cut out and fill in the capitalization worksheet.
  - You'll fold the flaps so that the printed words are on the outside. Lift the flap and write an example inside.

- The one side is a list of things you capitalize. The other side is a list of things you don't.
  - Capitalize: the first word in a sentence, the first word in a quote, the main words of a title, people's titles when used with their names or as their names, proper nouns (names of people, places, and things)
  - Don't Capitalize: common nouns, prepositions and insignificant words in titles, name titles (like president) if not used with names or as names, the seasons, directions (like north and south)

2. Organize your list of ten facts from Lesson 52 into three groups, three main topics. It's okay if you have to discard a fact that doesn't fit. The facts will become the details in your three topic paragraphs that will tell about the person's life.
   - One way to do it is to place a check mark next to three facts that go together and then a little circle next to another three that go together, etc. You could also color code to group the facts.
   - If you need to, find more facts so that you have at least two or three for each group.

3. Write one paragraph for your biography essay. You should type this one up. We'll be working on our essay over several days. Here's a reminder of what a paragraph should look like.
   - Main Idea
     - This sentence comes first and introduces what you'll be talking about in the paragraph.
   - Body
     - Use your facts to provide the details for this topical paragraph. This part gives the details. Teach your reader. Share an idea.
   - Conclusion
     - Finish with a sentence that sums it up. This is the last sentence in the paragraph.

Lesson 54
1. There is no worksheet for today. Read the comma rules.
   - Use a comma to separate things in a series.
   - Use a comma before a little conjunction (and, but, or, so) when they separate two independent clauses.
   - Use a comma to separate introductory words in a sentence.
   - Use a comma to section off unnecessary information.
   - Use a comma to separate adjectives if you could say "and" between them.
   - Use a comma to separate quotes from a speech tag.
   - Use a comma to separate phrases that express contrast.
   - Use a comma to avoid confusion.
   - Use a comma between city and state, and date and year.
   - Don't use only one comma between a subject and its verb.
2. Without looking, name as many as you can. There are 10.

3. Write two more paragraphs for your biography essay. These are the second and third paragraph for the body of your essay, the middle. These tell about the person you've chosen. Make sure they are in good paragraph form.
4. You should have included all of your information by the end of today's assignment.

Lesson 55

1. Write an example sentence for each comma rule in your workbook. You can look back at Lesson 31 if you need help with ideas.
2. Write a short dialogue between the person you chose for your biography essay and another historical character. What would George Washington and Abraham Lincoln have talked about? Neil Armstrong and Davy Crockett?

Lesson 56

1. You are going to be writing your introduction today, so let's talk about what makes a good one.
   - There are three key ingredients to an introductory paragraph.
     - The first is the opening sentence, your hook.
       - This needs to get the attention of the reader. You could use an interesting fact, a quotation, or a story, preferably humorous.
     - That is to be followed by a little information that builds towards your thesis.
     - That thesis is the most important part of your essay.
       - It is the point you are going to make with your essay.
       - Your whole essay should support the claim you made in your thesis.
   - Here are some examples from ThoughtCo.
     - Surprising fact: The pentagon has twice as many bathrooms as are necessary. The famous government building was constructed in the 1940s, when segregation laws required that separate bathrooms be installed for people of African descent. This building isn't the only American icon that harkens back to this embarrassing and hurtful time in our history. Across the United States there are many examples of leftover laws and customs that reflect the racism that once permeated American society.
     - Humor: When my older brother substituted fresh eggs for our hard-boiled Easter eggs, he didn't realize our father would take the first crack at hiding them. My brother's holiday ended early that particular day in 1991, but the rest of the family enjoyed the warm April weather, outside on the lawn, until late into the evening. Perhaps it was the warmth of the day and the joy of eating Easter roast while Tommy contemplated his actions that make my memories of Easter so sweet. Whatever the true reason, the fact is that my favorite holiday of the year is Easter Sunday.
     - Quotation: Hillary Rodham Clinton once said that "There cannot be true democracy unless women's voices are heard." In 2006, when Nancy Pelosi became the nation's first female Speaker of the House, one woman's voice rang out clear. With this development, democracy grew to its truest level ever in terms of women's equality. The historical event also paved the

way for Senator Clinton as she warmed her own vocal chords in preparation for a presidential race.

- https://www.thoughtco.com/the-introductory-paragraph-1857260

2. Write your introduction for your biographical essay. Remember that the last sentence of the paragraph is your topic sentence, your *thesis*. Make sure your essay body supports your thesis!

Lesson 57
1. Complete the comma worksheet in your workbook for today.
2. Write a short comedy dialogue. One idea would be to think of some misunderstanding where they are talking together but thinking about two different things.
   - An example from *Penrod*: Penrod's teacher thought he was talking to her, but he had been daydreaming and thinking of something else.

Lesson 58
1. There is no workbook page for today, but there are two things you have to do.
2. First, let's do a quick review of simple, compound, and complex sentences.
   - Simple - subject and predicate
     - My dog and I like to run and play.
     - My dog and I run around the house.
   - Compound - two sentences put together
     - I like to play with my dog, and my dog likes to play with me.
     - My dog is fun, but he is slobbery.
   - Complex - two subjects and predicates but not two sentences put together
     - I really like to play with my dog because my dog is so playful.
     - When I play with my dog, he looks like he's laughing.
   - Find one of each type of sentence in a book.
3. Today you will be writing your concluding paragraph for your biographical essay. Here's what you need to know about writing a conclusion.
   - There are three parts to the conclusion just like there are three parts to the introduction. The conclusion mirrors the introduction in reverse.
     - First, restate your thesis, but do it with different words.
     - Second, summarize your points from the body. You aren't introducing any new information here, and you aren't just repeating yourself.
     - Third, make an impression, convince the reader that what you were talking about matters, share your thoughts and feelings or push the reader to form thoughts and feelings on the subject.
       - Here's an example from Perdue.edu.
         - Getting a better job is a goal that I would really like to accomplish in the next few years. Finishing school will take me a long way to meeting this goal. To meet my goal, I will also prepare my résumé and search for jobs. My goal may not be an easy one to achieve, but things that are worth doing are often not easy.
           - https://owl.english.purdue.edu/engagement/2/2/60/

Lesson 59
1. Here is another set of sentence types.
   - Declarative - sentences that tell
     - I like my dog, but I don't like his drool.
   - Interrogative - sentences that ask
     - Why do I like my dog? Go and play with my dog. My dog's the best!
   - Imperative - sentences that command
     - Go and play with my dog. Go and play with my dog!
   - Exclamatory - sentences that exclaim
     - My dog's the best!
2. Practice identifying these sentence types with the activity in your workbook.

Lesson 60
1. In your workbook, write an advertisement for the (pretend) band the main character of your book is in, whatever you are reading. What would a commercial or magazine say about the band?
2. If you want, make a mini poster to advertise them.

Lesson 61
1. Now you are going to put all your essay paragraphs together. If they aren't typed, type them now if you can.
2. You need to add transitions between your paragraphs. You can't just jump from one idea to another. You need sentences like, "While George Washington was a great leader during times of war, he was also a great leader during times of peace." In the previous paragraph you talked about him as general; in the coming paragraph you will talk about him as president.
3. To help, here is a list of transition words.
   - in the first place, not only ... but also, as a matter of fact, as well as, although this may be true, on the other hand, with this in mind, in order to, in other words, for one thing, certainly, especially, for instance, to demonstrate, as a result, consequently, generally speaking, for the most part, in fact, in either case, ultimately, at the present time, to begin with
     - You can read hundreds more at SmartWords.org.
       - http://www.smart-words.org/linking-words/transition-words.html
   - Add words like these to connect your thoughts.

Lesson 62
1. Make sure in your biographical essay you have simple, compound, and complex sentences. You should try to have declarative, interrogative, and exclamatory sentences as well.
2. The more varied your sentences, the more interesting your essay. Work on editing your sentences to make them varied.

Lesson 63

1. Read your essay out loud. Note any parts that don't read easily. Fix them.
2. In a thesaurus, look up one noun, one adjective, and one verb in your essay. Replace them with a better word.
3. What better descriptions can you add?

Lesson 64

1. Use the checklist and mark it as you read through your essay. Fix any problems. Check for capital letters and commas. Fix any mistakes. Add a title. List at the bottom of your essay the information on the places where you got your facts.
2. Write a title at the top.
3. If you want to take part in peer editing, find someone around your age to read your essay. Give them the rubric.

Lesson 65

1. Write a letter to your mother as a character from the time period you are studying in history.
2. If you have to write in hieroglyphics, so be it.

Lesson 66

1. You'll be editing paragraphs in your workbook today.
2. If you want to refresh yourself on the comma rules, look back at Lesson 54 (and Lesson 31).

Lesson 67

1. Your workbook today is a Mad Libs activity. You write words without knowing the story, and then you read the words inserted into the story.
2. Take this book and place it over the bottom of the page in the workbook to hide the paragraph while you write your words. It will turn out better that way.
3. You'll be asked for different parts of speech. Here are a few that you may not know.
   - An ING verb is a verb in the form that ends with ING.
     - running instead of run
   - An exclamation is an expression you exclaim.
     - Oh! Golly! Wow! Ouch!
   - A past tense verb is a verb in the form it would be used in talking about something that already happened.
     - ran instead of run, fell instead of fall
   - A collective noun is when a lot of people or things are called by a singular name.
     - A team is made up of a lot of people but is one thing.
     - Traffic is made up of a lot of cars but is a singular noun.
     - A school of fish is made up of lots of fish, but it is "A" school, just one.

Lesson 68

1. Read the book report example on the following pages.
2. Read through the notes pointing out the different parts.
3. Write an introduction paragraph for a book report on a book you have recently finished reading. Include everything mentioned in the example: title, author, your feelings about

the book, summary, and thesis. The thesis is the topic sentence, the main idea of your report. What is it that you want to tell people about the book? Write it in the final sentence of your introduction. This is your thesis. Think of some examples from your book that show your main point and jot them down after your introductory paragraph to help you out when you have to write the next paragraphs.

4. This is something you should be typing. We'll work on this over several days.

Lesson 69
1. Write at least three example paragraphs. They should be about three to five sentences.
2. Make sure your first sentence of each paragraph tells what you will be talking about and uses a connection. The example uses the word "also" to connect the paragraphs.

Lesson 70
1. Reread the last paragraph of the example book report.
2. Write your conclusion. Make sure you restate your thesis in the first sentence using different wording. Make sure you include your thoughts or feelings about the topic. Write three to five sentences.
3. If you ever wrote three simple sentences in a row in your essay, change one to break up the sentence type/length.

Lesson 71
1. Use the editing guide in your workbook to check over your work.
2. Fix any problems you see.
3. Look at the example book report on the following pages and make sure you included everything you should have.
4. Read your book report essay out loud. Any place you stumble, change it.
5. Change it to make it better and to fix problems. Choose better words…make the sentences more interesting…
6. When you are finished, print it out and share it.
7. You might want to save this in your portfolio.

Find Lesson 72 on page 26.

The Voyage of the Dawn Treader

<u>The Voyage of the Dawn Treader, by C.S. Lewis</u>, is one of the <u>most moving and exciting</u> <u>books I have ever read</u>. Edmund and Lucy Pevensie, along with their unpleasant cousin Eustace, are transported through a painting of a ship from England to another world called Narnia, which Edmund and Lucy had visited before. They land in the sea and are taken up onto a Narnian ship, where Edmund and Lucy find their old friend Caspian, who is now King of Narnia. The three children accompany the ship and its crew on their quest through the unknown eastern seas. Caspian is seeking the seven Narnian lords who were exiled years before by his evil uncle, and also seeking to find the eastern edge of the world. The group undergoes many adventures and hardships on the islands they encounter on their quest. They do eventually find all of the missing lords, or discover how they died, and also find the end of the world. While the novel is an exciting story, it is also more than that. <u>The ideas of faith and</u> <u>redemption are all through the story</u>, making me feel that in a way the events of the story are tied in to real life.

Author name and book title
Your feelings about the book

Introduction includes book summary

Thesis

<u>The book is a story of faith in Aslan</u>. Edmund and Lucy always have faith in Aslan, a great talking lion who represents Jesus Christ in the Narnia stories. For example, Lucy is afraid to go into the mysterious magician's mansion on one of the islands, but she has to in order to find and say the spell that will make the Dufflepuds, the invisible inhabitants of the island, visible again. She trusts Aslan to take care of her and help her and even sees Aslan and talks with him in the mansion when she needs him most.

First point

Support from the book

At the end of the story, the children and a few of the others meet Aslan in person at the end of the world, which turns out to be the entrance to Aslan's country, like heaven. He sends Lucy and Edmund back to their own world, telling them they will never come back to Narnia. When they are upset and protest about never seeing him again, he tells them that they will get to know him by another name in their own world.

More evidence from the book

The book is also full of the idea of redemption, or being saved from something bad and or changed into something good. The most moving example was on one of the islands the ship landed on, where Eustace, who had been a complaining, stealing bully so far on the journey, finds a dragon's treasure, and gets magically turned into a dragon himself because of his greed. He lets the others know what happened, and is able to help them because of his new size and strength. Later Aslan comes and meets him and tears away his dragon skin and turns him into a boy again.

Second point

In the magician's mansion, Aslan saved Lucy from giving in to the temptation to say a spell which would make her beautiful. We learn that Lucy has been jealous of her sister Susan's beauty and almost says a spell which would have made her beautiful but also would have caused a lot of destruction. At that moment Aslan shows up and corrects and comforts Lucy, saving her from making a mistake which would have ended up causing a lot of pain.

Organized evidence from the book

The idea of faith and redemption run through the whole book. And although the book is full of magical events, talking animals, and exciting adventures, for me it still is very personal and real because these ideas are real in my life and my world. After all, the real main character of the book is Aslan, and he is in our world as well as in Narnia. He's just known by another name here.

Conclusion restates the thesis and summarizes your thoughts

Lesson 72

1. Try your hand at finding adjectives in these sentences in your workbook. Here's an example:
   - My one, sweet, adorable gray kitten sweater
   - Every word is an adjective except sweater. They are all describing the sweater. It's mine; it's the only one; it's sweet; it's adorable; it's gray; it's not just any kind of sweater, a kitten sweater.
   - Some people would call a basketball game a compound noun, but if you had to call just basketball something, it would be an adjective describing the game.
2. Here's a hint: look for nouns and then see if there are any words that describe that noun — in any way. Adjectives *almost* always come before a noun.
3. Save this in your portfolio.

Lesson 73

1. Write a letter to the president. Use a formal letter writing format.
2. In the top corner goes your address, then beneath it the date, then beneath that the name and address of who is getting your letter…look at the example letter for how to lay out your letter. Then write it!
3. Make sure you use a formal voice. It should sound respectful, not like you are talking to your little brother.

Lesson 74

1. Take this adjective quiz in your workbook and learn from any mistakes.
2. Think about the job of an adjective.
3. Hint: Think about what a proper noun is: Oreo as opposed to cookie. All proper nouns begin with a capital letter.

Lesson 75

1. Write a letter from a child from the time period you are studying. This is not a formal letter. You will use an informal voice, but it should still use proper grammar and spelling.
   - An informal voice is what you use to speak with family and friends. A formal voice is used to speak to those in authority or if you were writing to a business.
   - informal vs formal – hey and hi vs. hello and good afternoon
2. There's an example on the page to get the structure.

Lesson 76

1. We are going to be talking about advertising for several days. One job a writer can get is writing ads for companies. What's the purpose of an ad? To change your mind. They want to make you think a certain way, usually they want you to think you want to buy their item.
2. Here are some ad techniques that advertisers use.
   - Bandwagon
     - They want you to jump on the bandwagon. It's an expression that means, "Everyone else is doing it, so you should too." The ad tries to make it seem like everyone else already knows how great this is. What's taking you so long to join them?

- An example might be something like: Join the millions who have already switched to…
- Individuality
  - These ads encourage you to be unique. They appeal to the desire to be cool, stand out, celebrate your own style.
- Bait and switch
  - They lure you in with one thing, usually a bargain, and then sell you something expensive.
  - I see this often on websites. Get your free….and then you scroll and scroll trying to get to the end of it to get your free book or whatever, and then it says you can have all these others things as well, just pay…
  - Some people do this dishonestly and will say there is a bargain inside, but once you are in the store they say they're all out and offer you other more expensive alternatives.
- Celebrity spokesperson
  - People trust the celebrity and think if they use the product, it must be good.
- Plain folk
  - The opposite of celebrity, but with a similar impact, this approach shows how this product is used by regular folk, just like you. If they chose it, then it's good enough for you as well.
- Emotional appeals
  - These obviously appeal to your emotions, most recognizable are the ads that try to make you feel bad, like the ones about dogs who have been abused, send money to help these poor….
  - Most ads use emotion if they are good ads. They want to create a feeling of excitement or create a mood, like perfume ads. Another example is all those horrible medicine commercials. While they are listing all the ways it can kill you, they are showing happy families and trying to create an emotional response in you to override what your brain is hearing about all that could go wrong.
- Loaded Language
  - This is also used in most ads. It means using words that appeal to the emotions. They are called "purr words." Fresh, juicy, adventure, …
- Glittering Generalities
  - Related to these is the appealing to the emotions through a broad theme such as patriotism or world peace. They are invoking a feeling and hoping you connect that feeling to their product.
- Humor
  - This can be seen in the Geiko and Progressive ads. They are both for car insurance. They both only basically say that you can save money by using them, and they make you laugh.
- Comparison/name-calling
  - This can be comparing products showing that theirs is better, or just attacking the other product/person to show how they aren't as good.

3. On your worksheet today, you'll be identifying these techniques.

Lesson 77

1. Today you will be writing an ad. Here are the things you need to think about to make your ad effective.
    - What idea are you wanting to get across?
    - Who are you talking to? Who is your audience? Is your product for kids, for example?
    - What emotions or beliefs might reach that audience?
    - What people should be in your ad, considering the audience you want to reach?
    - What is your slogan, something that is catchy and easily memorable?
    - What ad techniques (more than one) will have the most impact on your audience?
2. Choose a product to write an ad for.
3. Write/draw/create an ad using the questions above to guide you to make an effective ad.

Lesson 78

1. Look at ads if you can, in newspapers, magazines, or online. What do you notice?
2. Complete the worksheet on advertising. The ad has a happy mother and child playing together and says Eat More Fruit and keep fit – The fruits of perfect health. Did you notice the size of the fruit in the fruit bowl?

Lesson 79

1. Today's worksheet is for analyzing commercials.
2. Watch two commercials on TV or online and make observations. (Note: There are two example commercials in lesson 79 in the online course, if you want to just use those.)

Lesson 80

1. Write a commercial based on what you've learned. Describe what people would see and what would be said.
2. Sell, sell, sell!
3. You might want to save this in your portfolio.

Lesson 81

1. You are going to be writing a humor piece, a funny story. Today you need to choose your main character.
2. Use your worksheet to draw a picture of your character and then write a description of your character. Make sure you give your character a name and age.
3. What about the character makes him or her funny?

Lesson 82

1. Practice parts of speech.
2. On your worksheet you'll be identifying how the words are used.
    - The same word can be used as different parts of speech.
        - He worked hard. Hard is an adverb describing how he worked. Work is a verb in that sentence.
        - That was hard work. Hard is an adjective describing the noun work.
    - The point is to pay attention to how a word is used.

3. Decide on the setting for your humorous story: the bedroom, the playground, the supermarket, the moon…
4. You can jot it down on your Lesson 81 page to make sure you don't forget.

Lesson 83
1. Think about a book that made you laugh. What events made it funny?
2. Decide what's going to happen in your story, beginning, middle, and end.
3. On your worksheet plan out the major flow of your story. What is going to make it funny?

Lesson 84
1. In your workbook there is another parts of speech practice page.
2. Start writing your humorous story. You'll finish in lesson 85. There is no page for this. It would be best to type this to save it to continue working on it.

Lesson 85
1. Finish writing your humorous story. There is no workbook page for today.
2. Read it to an audience. Did they laugh?

Lesson 86
1. On your worksheet for today, write a description of the main character of a book or story, maybe from a book you are currently reading for school.
2. Describe more than just how he or she looks. Write as much detail as you can think of, such as how do they act and what their likes and dislikes are.

Lesson 87
1. Today you are going to be choosing between homophones (words that sound the same but are spelled differently).
2. The easiest to identify are the contractions. Who's is just who is. The others you will have to recognize by their spelling.
3. Any answer you get wrong, write a sentence using the incorrect homophone you chose.

Lesson 88
1. The subject of a sentence is what the sentence is about. An object is part of a phrase.
   - I, you, he, she, it, we, they are subject pronouns. We use them as the subject of the sentence.
     - I did.
     - He did.
     - She and Angie did.
     - They did.
     - You and Marcus did.
   - Me, you, him, her, it, us, them are object pronouns. We use them as the object of a preposition and as direct and indirect objects that come after verbs.
     - Give it to Hope and me.
     - Hannah didn't mean to hurt you.
     - Paul is going with him.

- ▪ Take it from her.
- ▪ Don't do that around us.
- ▪ Benjamin is finding them.

2. Choose the correct pronouns on your worksheet. If the sentences are long or use a name along with the pronoun, shorten the sentence and take out extra words to help you realize which pronoun fits.
3. Don't forget to learn from any mistakes!

Lesson 89

1. You are going to be choosing pronouns again. This time there are possessive pronouns as well.
2. They show that something belongs to someone. They never use an apostrophe.
   - • That's my dog. It's mine.
   - • That's your dog. It's yours.
   - • That's her dog. It's hers.
   - • That's his dog. It's his.
   - • That's our dog. It's ours.
   - • That's their dog. It's theirs.
3. One use of the subject pronoun is after the word than, in most cases. When we speak, we often just say things like, "She's taller than me." No one blinks an eye at it. But technically, it should be taller than I. Think of it as saying, "She's taller than I am." You wouldn't say, "Me am." Then the subject pronoun makes sense.
4. On your worksheet you'll choose the correct pronoun. Learn from any mistakes!

Lesson 90

1. There's another pronoun practice in your workbook.
2. Here's a really tricky one.
   - • That's his playing you hear. NOT that's him playing you hear. The playing belongs to him. It's his playing.
3. Learn from any mistakes.

Lesson 91

1. You are going to be editing sentences on your worksheet for today.
2. Look for correct word choice along with spelling, grammar, and punctuation mistakes.

Lesson 92

1. You are going to be placing semicolons on your worksheet for today.
2. A semicolon replaces a period. Look for two independent clauses in the sentences on the page and separate them with a semicolon.

Lesson 93

1. You are going to be editing again on your worksheet for today. Editing your work is an essential step in writing.
2. There are a lot of spelling mistakes in your activity today. Trust your instincts when something catches your attention. If you stare at it enough, it may start to seem right. Pay

attention to when your mind signals a reaction that something isn't right. If you don't know the correct spelling, look it up in a dictionary.
3. Learn from any you missed. Your comma rules are in lesson 54 (and Lesson 31).

Lesson 94
1. On your worksheet today, you'll be doing a little spelling activity first.
2. Then you will be playing Mad Libs. Use this book to cover up the bottom of the page to make it more interesting.

Lesson 95
1. There is an editing exercise today.
2. Learn from any you missed. Make sure you understand why it is what it is.

Lesson 96
1. You are going to be writing a persuasive essay. That's an essay that is written with the intention of persuading someone, changing their mind, causing them to think the way you do on an issue.
2. Today you need to choose a topic. You need to read an article on the issue or interview someone on their opinion. You should do research for this essay, so it would be easiest to choose a topic you can look up online.
3. If you read *Black Beauty*, animal rights are brought up in the book. Online in the Language Arts 6 course in lesson 96, you can find a link to read an article on animal cruelty.
4. Today in your workbook, write a paragraph comparing and contrasting your feelings about your topic and the other person's perspective on the topic.

Lesson 97
1. Fill in what you can on the FIRES chart by researching your topic.
   - For example: One topic can be mistreatment of chickens today. The third topic could be a "counter argument," an argument why we don't need to or shouldn't worry about animal rights–that could be that prices would go up if their techniques changed.
   - Fill in the rest of the chart as best as you can. (You don't have to fill in every box, but you'll want to have at least one of each kind of box filled in, meaning you should have at least one statistic, etc.)
2. In the online course for this day, you can find links to articles about animal cruelty.

Lesson 98
1. Read the example of a persuasive essay on the following page.
2. Write an introduction and your two reasons for a persuasive essay based on this example and your chart from lesson 97.
3. There's no workbook page for this. Type it if you can. You'll be working on this through Lesson 100.

Say No to Cell Phones

What do you see when you look at a crowd of people? You probably see the majority of them on their cell phones. What don't you see? People interacting, talking to one another, greeting each other, saying hi to a stranger. Being friendly to each other is a nice thing, but there are more important reasons to put the phone down. Cell phones literally hurt us as they hijack our brains and create anxiety.

> Variety of sentence structures
>
> Introduction sets a scene
>
> Thesis states two reasons

First, cell phone hijack our brains. They send signals to our brains that create an addiction. There are people who have even developed a condition where they feel their cell phone vibrate even when nothing is happening. Cell phones consume our thoughts, causing dangerous distractions. Accidents of any kind are more likely when you are on a phone. The risk of getting hit by a car goes up more than 40% when you are on a cell phone while walking across the street.

> First reason
>
> Facts to support reason one

These accidents are even more deadly when it's the driver who is on the phone. In fact, texting when driving is "by far the most alarming distraction" according to the US government, comparing it to driving while drunk.

> Expert quote to support reason

Cell phones don't just distract, they cause anxiety. They cause a feeling that you have to check your messages and that you have to respond right away. When there are no messages, it can cause depression. Even worse, it is estimated that one out of every three teenagers experiences cyberbullying, people saying hurtful things to them online. They are exposed to this through social media apps on cell phones which gives harassers constant and private access.

> Second reason
>
> Transitions show organization
>
> Support for second reason

According to research, the more time someone spends looking at their phones, the more depressed they feel. According to researcher Twenge, "There's not a single exception." This is true for people of all ages.

> Facts/quote/specifics

It can be argued that cell phones are necessary. They connect us. They give us answers. They help us find our way. However, phones can be used to complete specific tasks and then put away the rest of the time. Social media can also be used for a specific purpose and at a set time without relying on it for interaction and friendship.

> Counterargument
>
> Response (not argumentative)

Do you want to make a change? Encourage children and parents to say no to cell phones until they become more necessary, like when a child gets a job. Set an example by putting down your phone and having fun with friends and family. Make the healthy choice for yourself and encourage others to follow your good example.

> Conclusion and call to action

Lesson 99

1. Using the example, write your counterargument section and conclusion.
2. Present the count argument in a fair way. There are real reasons why people believe differently on subjects.
3. Make sure your essay is complete.

Lesson 100

1. Edit your essay.
2. Fill out a critique of your essay using the worksheet in your workbook.
3. Publish your essay when you are ready.
4. Save this in your portfolio.

Lesson 101

1. Today you are editing sentences.
2. There are a bunch of homophones, words that sound the same but are spelled differently. If you are reading and it doesn't make sense, it probably needs a different word in there.
3. Also, be on the lookout for punctuation mistakes and missing quotation marks. Don't forget your lessons on pronoun choice!

Lesson 102

1. This sentence is in your workbook.
   - One smooth path led into the meadow, and here the little folk congregated; one swept across the pond, where skaters were darting about like water-bugs; and the third, from the very top of the steep hill, ended abruptly at a rail fence on the high bank above the road. (from *Jack and Jill*, by Alcott)
2. It is describing three different sledding paths the children could take. The first was for the smaller children. Look at the punctuation. There is a list of three sledding paths. The list is divided by semi-colons, not commas.
3. On your worksheet, circle the first comma. What is its function? It is needed because before and after the comma are two **independent clauses**; they could both be complete sentences. "One smooth path led into the meadow." "Here the little folk congregated." The comma always comes before the conjunction, e.g. and, or, but, so.
4. When you are listing things and use commas within the listed items, then you use semi-colons to separate the items on your list. Normally, you would use commas to separate items in a list.
   - "One smooth path led into the meadow, and here the little folk congregated;"
   - There is a comma in the middle of the first item on the list, so we need a semi-colon after it before we list the next thing.
5. Underline all the verbs. She uses great verbs that describe, not just tell, what the characters are doing.
   - How is "swept" across the pond better than "goes" across the pond?
   - How is "darting" about better than "moving" about?
6. Circle the next comma.
   - "one swept across the pond, where skaters were darting about like water bugs;"

- This comma separates off unnecessary information. The author is saying that kind of as an aside, she's not really giving us information on which pond as if we'd be confused if she didn't clarify. She's just adding a description.

7. "Skaters were darting about like water bugs" is a simile. Skaters are being compared to water bugs using like or as.

8. Write a simile describing skaters. There's a space on your worksheet.

9. Circle the next two commas. These two are a pair. The sentence could be, "And the third ended abruptly at a rail fence…" She adds in a description of the third.

10. Now, you write a list of three things you are going to do today. Write them on every other line so that you have room to add words. You might want to use a pencil for this. There may be erasing involved!
    - e.g. Today I'm going to wake up, make my bed, and drink a cup of tea.

11. Now add a comma to each thing on your list. (You'll need to add words.) You'll also need to add semi-colons.
    - e.g. Today I'm going to wake up, not that I have a choice; make my bed, if tossing back my covers can count; and drink a cup of tea, a warm, lovely cup of tea.

12. Now, add a simile.
    - e.g. Today I'm going to wake up, not that I have a choice; make my bed, if tossing back my covers like a Matador whipping around his bull cape counts; and drink a cup of tea, a warm, lovely cup of tea.

Lesson 103

1. This paragraph is in your workbook for today.
   - "Well, no; it usually takes twenty-one days for bones to knit, and young ones make quick work of it," answered the doctor, with a last scientific tuck to the various bandages, which made Jack feel like a hapless chicken trussed for the spit. (from *Jack and Jill*, by Alcott)

2. Circle the quotation marks. Quotation marks go around whatever someone is saying. Whenever a new speaker begins, a new paragraph starts.

3. Circle the first comma. This comma comes after an introductory exclamation.
   - Examples: Well, Yes, No, Actually…

4. Circle the semi-colon. This is used as a period. You could use a period there. Semi-colons are used a lot more in older writing than in modern writing.

5. Circle the next comma. This again separates two **independent clauses**. What are the two clauses that could stand alone as their own sentences?

6. Circle the next comma and quotation marks. You always use a comma instead of a period when closing out a quote before a **speech tag**, like *Susan said*. You are allowed to use exclamation points and question marks, though. The punctuation always comes before the quotation marks.

7. Circle the next two commas. Here we see again the sectioning off of additional information. These are **dependent clauses**, meaning they couldn't be their own sentence. "With a last scientific tuck to the various bandages" doesn't work as a sentence.

8. In the last **clause** we read another simile: "made Jack feel like a hapless chicken trussed for the spit." Here is a before and after picture of a chicken trussed for the spit. Do you see that there is string on it, squeezing it together?

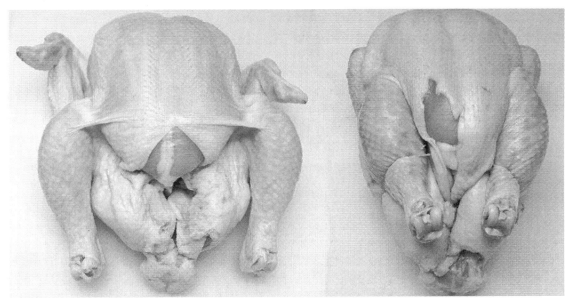

9. Your turn. Write a comment someone is saying. Start on the second line.
    - e.g. "I'll be home by noon," she said as she walked out the door.
10. Add an introductory expression (and comma.)
    - e.g. "Wait, no, change of plans, I'll be home by noon," she said as she walked out the door.
11. Add a conjunction and independent clause to your quote.
    - e.g. "Wait, no, change of plans, I'll be home by noon, or I'll call you," she said as she walked out the door.
12. Add a comma and additional description to the end of your sentence.
    - e.g. "Wait, no, change of plans, I'll be home by noon, or I'll call you," she said as she walked out the door, letting it slam behind her.
13. Now add a simile.
    - e.g. "Wait, no, change of plans, I'll be home by noon, or I'll call you," she said as she walked out the door, letting it slam behind her like the crash of thunder when the storm is near.
14. Make sure you have all your commas and quotation marks.
    Answers: #5 It usually takes twenty-one days for bones to knit. Young ones make quick work of it.

Lesson 104
1. What is something, other than food, that you would describe as delicious? Louisa May Alcott uses the word to describe a couch.
2. In your workbook, write a great sentence using the word delicious describing your answer to number one.

Lesson 105
1. Use a book you are reading to spy out and copy down 5 nouns, 5 verbs, 5 adjectives and 5 pronouns. There are spots for them on your worksheet today.
    - hint: herself, yourself, etc. are pronouns
2. Use long sentences to write a short story about what you would do for amusement if you were stuck in bed.

Lesson 106

1. Alcott's second paragraph in chapter five of *Jack and Jill* is just one sentence. It contains more than eighty words! Let's write a long sentence together.

2. Let's start with one piece of the structure of her sentence. You will write a sentence starting with when. Read all about that type of sentence below.
   - After the first **clause**, you will put a comma. A **when clause** is a dependent clause. It can't stand as its own sentence.
     - *When I get up in the morning, my bones creak and crackle.*
     - The phrase "when I get up in the morning" is not a sentence by itself. It is "dependent" on the rest of the sentence.
   - The second part of the sentence is an **independent clause**; it can stand alone as a sentence.
     - "My bones creak and crackle."
   - When we pair the two together, you get a **complex** sentence. Remember those?

3. Now, you do it. Write a complex sentence. Start out with "When…," Don't forget the comma! Start on 2nd line.

4. Now let's add in a first part to the sentence, followed by a *but*.
   - An independent clause followed by a comma and a conjunction (such as but) followed by another independent clause is a **compound** sentence.
   - Alcott compounds a complex sentence. Let's try.
     - *At night I sleep peacefully, but when I get up in the morning, my bones creak and crackle.*

5. You give it a try.

6. Now we are nowhere near eighty words yet, but we have a good start. Take a look at her sentence. It's a whole paragraph in the book.

   Great plans had been afoot for Christmas or New Year, but when the grand catastrophe put an end to the career of one of the best "spouters," and caused the retirement of the favorite "singing chambermaid," the affair was postponed till February, when Washington's birthday was always celebrated by the patriotic town, where the father of his country once put on his nightcap, or took off his boots, as that ubiquitous hero appears to have done in every part of the United States.

7. Do you see the **independent clause** that starts it, ending with "Year", the *but when* and the **dependent clause**, ending with "chambermaid" followed by a comma? Then there is one more **independent clause**, ending with "February." That is how far we have gone in copying the structure of this sentence.

8. What's next? She says, "when Washington's birthday was always celebrated by the patriotic town," describing February.

9. So, it's our turn. We are going to add on a description to the end of our last word/phrase.
   - *At night I sleep peacefully, but when I get up in the morning, my bones creak and crackle like an old board in a slow-burning fire.* I didn't do it just her way. See what you can come up with.

10. Now one last time. She adds, "where the father of his country once put on his nightcap, or took off his boots, as that ubiquitous hero appears to have done in every part of the United States." This is describing the last word from the phrase before, "town."

11. Alright, let's see if we can add one more descriptive phrase. *e.g. At night I sleep peacefully, but when I get up in the morning, my bones creak and crackle like an old board in a slow burning fire that's been drying in the shed waiting for its moment to shine.* Now you try.

12. How many words did you end up with? I got 39. I am trying to lengthen your sentences, but it's not just about how many words, it's about mixing up the structure of your sentences. It will make your writing more sophisticated and more interesting to read.

13. Think of an event in your life that you'd like to write a story about. You aren't writing today, just thinking about it.

14. There is a spelling activity. You can try to guess at the words, but you can also have someone read you the words from the answer key. You could also use it to play hangman.

Lesson 107

1. Write about Christmas day on your worksheet for today, even if you don't celebrate Christmas. (I certainly have memories of Ramadan from living in Turkey.)

2. Use long and varied sentences.

Lesson 108

1. There is a spelling activity in your workbook for today.

2. Read the examples of autobiographical incident that follows before you start writing yours. You'll be typing this one if you can because we'll be working on it over several days.

3. In your essay you'll want to think about including these elements.
   - Introduction and conclusion that show the meaning of the incident
   - Dialogue to show personalities
   - Sensory details (sight, sound, smell)
   - Transitions that show the order that things happened and to connect thoughts
   - A variety of sentence lengths

4. Write the introduction, dialogue and summary — first three to five paragraphs — following the example you read.

5. Make sure you start out with an interesting first sentence. One way to do that is by talking directly to the reader.

Visiting Nature

If you don't have a rural address, you don't get the daily chance to experience nature. Being surrounded by nature was what it was like at my grandparents' house in Rolla, Missouri. They had over a hundred acres, much of which they gave to a Bible camp, but when you were at their house, you could see nothing around but nature. While their house was fun to explore, the memory of the view is what still inspires me.

My grandparents had horses, and it was the only time I ever got to ride one. My grandpa led us to the paddock through a sea of grasses, lifted us gently onto Chestnut's back, and guided us around in the yard. We felt on top of the world on her broad back, towering above our parents.

We gave the horses saltlicks and fed them carrots. Chestnut was chestnut in color but had a white diamond on her forehead. She was my favorite horse, but probably just because she's the one we got to ride.

The trek to the paddock wasn't the only one we made. Their driveway was a quarter of a mile long. "We're going to walk a mile a day," my dad announced, deciding for the family. We walked up and back the long driveway morning and evening to make it a mile. We didn't mind. The driveway went through woods, and what kid doesn't love exploring in the woods? While my parents stuck to the path, we wove in and out of the trees, picking up sticks and stones and spotting animals that scurried for safety away from our excited feet.

We didn't just love the woods, we loved it all, except for the bugs. Chiggers clung to us and were picked off one by one. Once I slipped on my shoe only to find I had squished a grasshopper. I took to checking my shoes before I put them on after that. At night we lay awake, unable to sleep because of the noise of the crickets. The night noises were nothing like in suburbia.

But before nightfall came sunset. "Come and look," my mom called to my brother and I, and we crowded the picture window to see the setting sun. We looked out and saw nothing but grass, trees, and open sky. The sky was filled with the oranges and reds that mark the ending to a perfect day. The sunsets were beautiful, and so is the memory of them.

Lesson 109
1. You know adjectives describe nouns. Numbers and even words like *a* and *the* are used as adjectives.
2. Words like *that* can be adjectives. Which cat? That cat.
3. Here's another kind of adjective, participle adjectives. They are all forms of verbs
   - the *fallen* tree
   - the *spilled* milk
   - he is *fascinating*
   - she was *frustrated*
4. Do today's worksheet on this different type of adjective, participle adjectives.

Lesson 110
1. "In a moment Ralph was as meek as a Quaker, and sat looking about him with a mildly astonished air, as if inquiring the cause of such unseemly mirth."
2. *As meek as a Quaker* is a simile. Similes compare two unlike things using like or as. Later in the sentence there is an *as if*.
3. In your workbook, *write* a sentence with an *as/as* and an *as/if*.
   - e.g. *It was as hot as a pancake on the griddle, but my brother was running around like a maniac, as if he weren't already hot enough.*
4. Now write a short story with your first sentence being the one you just wrote.

Lesson 111
1. Write out these spelling words in your workbook.
   - beautifully, disastrous, policy, vacuum, numerator, headache, freight, arithmetic, calendar, horizon, vegetable, scissors, passenger, marriage, capacity, ceiling
2. Now go back and check them all to make sure they are correct. Rewrite any incorrect words so that you practice writing it correctly.

3. Now, let's move on to writing. We're going to write a sentence like this one.
   - "While Jack was hopping gayly about on his crutches, poor Jill was feeling the effects of her second fall, and instead of sitting up, as she hoped to do after six weeks of rest, she was ordered to lie on a board for two hours each day."
4. First step. Start with a **dependent clause** starting with "while." Don't forget to follow it with a comma. Then add an **independent clause**, one that could stand alone as a sentence. Start on the first line but maybe skip every other line as you write to add more in.
   - Example: *While I was waiting, a dog came up to sniff my shoes.*
5. Next, Alcott uses a comma and a conjunction (, and). Let's skip that part for now.
6. The second part of her sentence starts with another **dependent clause** (which I believe is specifically called an adverbial phrase, but you don't need to know that.) That's followed by an aside, an extra description. Then the sentence is finished with an **independent clause.**
7. Right now, let's write a dependent clause followed by an independent clause. Don't forget to separate the two with a comma. And remember this has to go with your first sentence.
   - Example: *Until he was satisfied that I wasn't the source of whatever scent he was chasing, he eagerly circled me.*
8. Now, add in a clause after the first comma and make sure to use a comma after it. Alcott added there, "as she hoped to do after six weeks of rest."
   - Example: *Until he was satisfied that I wasn't the source of whatever scent he was chasing, as he obviously was after something, he eagerly circled me.*
9. Now, we have to combine the two together. Use a comma and a conjunction between the two sentences you just wrote.
   - Example: *While I was waiting, a dog came up to sniff my shoes, and until he was satisfied that I wasn't the source of whatever scent he was chasing, as he obviously was after something, he eagerly circled me.*
10. Add a participle adjective and maybe a metaphor or simile. You can do it!
    - *Example: While I was waiting, a dog came up to sniff my shoes, and until he was satisfied that I wasn't the source of whatever scent he was chasing, as he obviously was after something, he eagerly circled me, a <u>frozen</u> statue on the corner of 24th and Main.* (I underlined my participle adjective. I added the metaphor of comparing myself to a statue.)

Lesson 112
1. In your workbook there are more blanks for spelling words. You can try to guess at the words today since you just saw them in lesson 111. This is a practice of those words.
2. If you can't guess some of them, you can find someone to play hangman with those words as you try to figure them out.
3. Work on writing the body of your autobiographical incident.
4. Think about all our writing practice. Try and include a simile, multiple clauses with added descriptions, and even a new word you've learned.

Lesson 113

1. In your workbook write a short one act play, just a single vignette like Washington cutting down the cherry tree.
2. On your script you will write the dialogue as well as describe the action. Here is an example of what a script looks like.

Deng: Well, oh Emperor. We are very poor. Our family could use a bigger home.

Emperor: A home? Done! (clap, clap)

Chin: (hands Deng a scroll)

Chou: And a larger property to farm.

Emperor: More land? Done! (clap, clap)

Lu: (hands Chou a scroll)

Li: And more money.

Emperor: Gold and wealth? Done! (clap, clap)

Han: (hands Li a scroll)

Jiang: And we would like to be able to go to school and perhaps train for the imperial guards.

Emperor: Education and position? Done! (clap, clap)

Chin: (hands Jiang a scroll)

Yan: And oh generous and spontaneous emperor, would you mind telling our parents that we have done something important?

Lesson 114

1. Another type of adjective is the **relative clause**.
2. They follow relative pronouns such as who, whom, whose, that, and which. Or, they follow a relative adverb such as when, where, and why.
3. These clauses describe. They are used as adjectives.
   - The girl over there, <u>who has on the red shirt</u>, she's the one you need to ask.
   - That car, <u>which looks like it's seen better days</u>, has been sitting here for weeks.
   - At noon, <u>when it's time for lunch</u>, we'll all meet back here.
4. I underlined each relative clause. Can you see how they are used as adjectives? What nouns are they describing?
5. In your workbook there is a word search to complete for today.
   Answers #4: girl, car, noon

Lesson 115

1. Find someone to help you with your spelling test. The words are in the back in the answer key.
2. Then come back and look at this sentence.
   - Jack understood, and, hopping across the room, gave both the thin hands a hearty shake; then, not finding any words quite cordial enough in which to thank this faithful little sister, he stooped down and kissed her gratefully. (from *Jack and Jill*, by Alcott)

3. I'm going to pull out two parts of the sentence. I'm going to chop it up and edit a little for ease of use.
   - Hopping across the room, he gave her a hearty handshake. Not finding any words, he kissed her gratefully.
4. She, of course, used a lot more words and combined them all into one long sentence. This time I just want to point out this sentence structure. Here's the structure: **participle phrase** – comma – subject described in the **participle phrase** – rest of sentence including predicate (verb).
5. IMPORTANT PARTS: comma after the opening phrase and the next word has to be the subject described in the phrase
6. **Hopping** across the room, **he** gave her a hearty handshake. Not **finding** any words, **he** kissed her gratefully.
7. I put in bold the participles and the subjects they modify (describe).
8. Write two sentences with this structure.
   - Examples: *Drying my hair, I hung my head upside while helping my three-year old on his quest to know why.*
   - *Knowing the answer, I raised my hand.*
9. Work on your autobiographical incident. Finish the body. Make sure you use a variety of sentence structures. Use at least one sentence that starts with a participle phrase. Use at least one relative clause.

Lesson 116
1. Take the Lesson 115 spelling test again if you got more than two wrong. If you got one or two wrong, try just those words again.
2. Read this sentence from *Jack and Jill*.
   - Then, having shaken hands heartily, Mr. Acton went away, and Jack flew off to have rejoicings with Jill, who sat up on her sofa, without knowing it, so eager was she to hear all about the call. (Alcott)
2. Let's look at the structure of this sentence. It's a **compound** sentence because of the **conjunction** "and" in the middle with an **independent** clause on both sides of it. That means you could split the sentence in two and both sides would work as sentences.
3. Let's look at the first half. "Then, **having shaken** hands heartily, **Mr. Acton** went away." Let's just pretend that's a sentence for now. This is what we talked about the last day, **participle** phrases. I put in bold the participle and who it modifies.
4. Remember, that the **participle phrase** must be followed by a comma and immediately by the subject it modifies. "Having shaken hands" is talking about what Mr. Acton was doing, so he has to come right after the comma. If it doesn't, it's called a dangling participle. It just dangles there not attached to anything. All alone. That's sad and that's bad. Don't do it.
5. Write a sentence in this structure, starting with a participle phrase.
   - e.g. *Waking to the alarm, I sat up abruptly.*
6. Now, let's look at the second part of the sentence.
   - Jack flew off to have rejoicings with Jill, **who sat up on her sofa**, without knowing it, so eager was she to hear all about the call.
     - I put in bold the **relative clause**. Remember those from a couple of days ago?

7. Let's ignore "without knowing it" and write a sentence with a relative clause. We're going to attach it to your last sentence to continue the thought.
    - e.g. *I tugged at the covers,* **which seem to have wrestled me in the night,** *and slipped from the bed.*
8. Now put them together with a conjunction. Don't forget the comma before the conjunction!
    - e.g. *Waking to the alarm, I sat up abruptly, and I tugged at the covers, which seem to have wrestled me in the night, and slipped from the bed.*
9. Work on your autobiographical incident. Write the conclusion.

Lesson 117

1. Write down these words in your workbook. These are the new words you'll be learning to spell, so pay attention to how they are spelled!
    - chrome, oxygen, interested, decrease, foliage, difficulty, cantaloupe, sensitive, zealous, laughter, opposite, imply, beguiled, archaeologist, parliament, jealousy
2. Let's look at this sentence.
    - It was impossible to refuse the invitation he had been longing for, and in they went to the great delight of Roxy, who instantly retired to the pantry, smiling significantly, and brought out the most elaborate pie in honor of the occasion. (from *Jack and Jill*, by Alcott)
2. What do you see in this sentence that we've been talking about?
3. What are the two independent clauses?
4. What conjunction connects them?
5. What is the relative clause?
6. Write a sentence following the same structure. Make sure you include a relative clause.
7. Edit your autobiographical incident. Look at your transitions. Look at your sentence structures.

    Answers: #2 compound sentence, relative clause #3 "It was impossible to refuse the invitation he had been longing for" and "in they went to the great delight of Roxy, who instantly retired to the pantry, smiling significantly, and brought out the most elaborate pie in honor of the occasion." #4 and #5 who instantly retired to the pantry

Lesson 118

1. There's a spelling activity in your workbook. Use it to help you think about how these words are spelled.
1. There are also lines for writing. Let's look at the commas in this sentence from *Jack and Jill*.
    - "Now, my dears, I've something very curious to tell you, so listen quietly and then I'll give you your dinners," said Molly, addressing the nine cats who came trooping after her as she went into the shed-chamber with a bowl of milk and a plate of scraps in her hands. (Alcott)
2. We start with quotes because someone is talking.
3. After the word "now," there is a comma. We put a comma after an introductory element.
    - Examples: Now, Yes, So, Because of his insistence, After the snow stops falling,…

4. We also put a comma after "now" because there are commas around "my dears." We put commas around a person's name, even if it isn't a proper name, as in this case, when we are addressing that person.
   - Examples: "Mom, could you…" "Also, Tim, I need…" You only use a comma if you are talking to the person.
5. Of course, we don't put two commas after "now." One comma is enough for both situations.
6. There is a comma before the **conjunction** "so." In a compound sentence, you always put a comma before the **conjunction**. (for, and, nor, but, or, yet, so — FANBOYS — acronym for all the conjunctions)
7. Then there is a comma after "dinners" because it is followed by a **speech tag** (in this case, said Molly).
8. We have one final comma after Molly, separating the **participle phrase** modifying "Molly." The sentence could be flipped. *Addressing the nine cats, Molly said, "Now, my dears, I've something to tell you."* I shortened it a bit. Alcott uses the participle at the end and uses a comma. Current rules (yes, they change) would say there shouldn't be a comma there because the **participle** directly follows the word it modifies, the word it describes.
9. You will see that although there are rules of grammar and punctuation, some of it is subjective and can be suited to the author. Some of it is NOT SUBJECTIVE, so stick to the rules as best you can!
10. Write a sentence following this structure.
    - e.g. *"Today, my beloved children, we are going to play a game," I said, laughing at their excitement.* (Note: I used "I said" so the participle wouldn't directly follow the word it modifies so that I could use a comma. Here it is commaless.) *"Today, my beloved children, we are going to play a game," said their mother laughing at their excitement.* Personally, I like the comma.
11. In your sentence make sure you address someone, my dears! Your sentence should have all the commas hers does except you decide how to structure your **speech tag** to use a comma or not before your **participle phrase.**
12. Edit your autobiographical incident. Check capitals, commas, spelling.
13. Read it out loud and fix any places that don't seem right.
14. Publish.
15. Save this in your portfolio.

Lesson 119

1. In your workbook you will find a spelling activity and a short practice on the parts of speech.
2. We're also going to look at another sentence from *Jack and Jill*.
   - With the help of the brace she could sit up for a short time every day, and when the air was mild enough she was warmly wrapped and allowed to look out at the open window into the garden, where the gold and purple crocuses were coming bravely up, and the snowdrops nodded their delicate heads as if calling to her, "Good day, little sister, come out and play with us, for winter is over and spring is here."

3. We start with an **independent clause**. "With the help of the brace she could sit up for a short time every day." It is independent because it can stand alone. It could be its own sentence, but Alcott loves long sentences!
4. Today, we would use a comma after brace, after an introductory phrase.
5. Next, we have a **comma** followed by a **conjunction**.
6. Then, we have a **when dependent clause**. We would today follow that with a **comma** (after "enough").
7. That is followed by an **independent clause,** "she was warmly wrapped and allowed to look out at the window into the garden."
8. We have a **phrase next which modifies** (or describes) "garden." That is unnecessary information and is set off by **commas**.
9. We have a **comma** to set off a quotation.
10. We have a **personal address** set off in **commas**.
11. In the quote itself we have a **compound sentence** with the conjunction "for," the "f" in FANBOYS.
12. Now you write a sentence with a similar structure using everything I wrote in bold in order. There are lines in your workbook for this.
    - e.g. *I sit at my computer every day*, **but** <u>when I think about how much time I've spent in that chair,</u> *I sigh a big sigh*, **acknowledging the magnitude of it,** <u>and I think,</u> *"Self,* **you best be getting up out of that chair,** <u>for your days are numbered.</u>*"* Use all the parts!

Lesson 120
1. Find someone to help you take the spelling test.
2. Practice with participles today. A participle is a verb used as an adjective. It can be in different tenses: the fallen tree – having fallen, the tree. It can even be used in the infinitive. An example would be, "That's the movie to watch." The verb to watch is describing, telling which movie.
3. There are two pages in your workbook today. The participles are on the second page. To help you find the participle, remember that they are adjectives and adjectives describe nouns, so look for the nouns.

Lesson 121
1. Take a look at this sentence.
    - "How is the old fellow?" called Frank from the boat, while Gus stood leaning on an oar in a nautical attitude. (Alcott, *Jack and Jill*)
2. Notice the lowercase "c" in called.
3. This is a **complex sentence** because the first part of the sentence is an **independent clause**, and the second part is a **dependent clause**–it couldn't be a sentence by itself.
4. Write a sentence in your workbook using this structure. Use a question as a quotation, a lowercase word after the quotes, and "while." Sometimes you use a comma before while and sometimes you don't. Modern usage says not to use a comma when you are using it to mean at the same time. Other rules can apply, though, such as unnecessary information.
5. Here's my example:
    - *"What are you doing?" my son asked from the doorway while I was crawling around the floor looking for my lost pin.*

6. See if you can do the adverb/adjective activity in your workbook.
7. Retake the spelling test from Lesson 120 IF you got more than two wrong. If you got one or two wrong, retry those words. Can you spell them correctly now?

Lesson 122

1. In your workbook, write a sentence in the fashion of the following sentence.
   - "Oh, when can I go out? I can't wait long," she said, looking as eager as a little gull shut up in a cage and pining for its home on the wide ocean. (Alcott, *Jack and Jill*, edited to shorten)
2. First, let's look at the quotation. Start with an introductory word and comma. You don't have to use a question. Your quote can just be one sentence and end with a comma this time.
   - Example: *"Yes, I think she is coming today,"*
3. Follow the quotes with a lowercase word (meaning, don't use a name) and then a comma.
   - Example: *"Yes, I think she is coming today," he said.*
4. Here is a participle phrase using a simile (comparing two unlike things using like or as). Jill is being compared to a gull shut up in a cage and longing for the ocean.
   - Example: *"Yes, I think she is coming today," he said, looking as unsure as most contestants on "Are You Smarter Than a Fifth Grader?"*
5. Now put your sentence into a short story.

Lesson 123

1. Read this excerpt.
   - Her back was turned to Jill, but something in the long brown braid with a fly-away blue bow hanging down her back looked very familiar to Jill. So did the gray suit and the Japanese umbrella; but the hat was strange, and while she was thinking how natural the boots looked, the girl turned round.
     "Why, how much she looks like Molly! It can't be–yes, it might, I do believe it is!" cried Jill, starting up and hardly daring to trust her own eyes. (Alcott, *Jack and Jill*)
2. In the second paragraph, look at the hyphen (–) and see how it is used in this case.
3. The hyphen in the first sentence is used in a different way. Since we have been looking at adjectives, I wanted to point it out, "fly-away blue."
4. The noun is bow. It's a blue bow. "Fly-away" describes the color of blue. It's not away blue and also fly blue. It's fly-away blue, meaning the color of a clear sky.
   - Here's another example.
     - That was the second-best thing I heard all day.
       - Second doesn't describe the thing he heard; best doesn't describe the thing he heard.
       - It wasn't the second thing, nor the best thing, but the second-best thing.
5. Let's write long adjectives. Remember, this is different than saying "big enormous cheery red house." Each of those adjectives is describing house. (One test is to say "and" between each adjective. If it still makes sense, then they don't get a hyphen.)

6. When we write hyphenated adjectives (adjectives linked with hyphens), the words together are one adjective.
7. In your workbook write a two-word adjective with a noun. Example: *small-town girl* She's not a town girl and a small girl; she's a small-town girl.
8. Make it longer. (If you need to, write a whole new one.) Example: *small-town-never-been-to-the-city girl*
9. Make it longer. Example: *born-and-raised-in-a-small-town-never-even-been-to-the-city-before kind of girl*
10. More examples: *deer-in-the-headlights look   tantrum-throwing two-year-old boy*
11. Take your adjective and put it in a short story.

Lesson 124

1. Take a look at this selection.
   - A thousand things came up as they sewed together in the afternoon, and the eager minds received much general information in an easy and well-ordered way. Physiology was one of the favorite studies, and Mrs. Hammond often came in to give them a little lecture, teaching them to understand the wonders of their own systems, and how to keep them in order– a lesson of far more importance just then than Greek or Latin, for girls are the future mothers, nurses, teachers, of the race, and should feel how much depends on them. Merry could not resist the attractions of the friendly circle, and soon persuaded her mother to let her do as they did; so she got more exercise and less study, which was just what the delicate girl needed. (Alcott, *Jack and Jill*)
2. What is the hyphenated adjective in the above selection?
3. How is the other hyphen used?
4. Do you remember how a semi-colon is used?
5. I won't make you copy this whole structure, but can you write a sentence with all three of these punctuation marks?
6. Here's my example:
   - *I'm tired, end-of-the-day tired, with still hours to go in front of me–not that I'm complaining; I'm grateful I have the strength to sit and type and even think, a little.*
   - Go for it!

Answers: #2 well-ordered, #3 It marks off an aside comment that's important. #4 like a period

Lesson 125

1. Complete the two pages of English review in your workbook.
2. You can look back in this book for reminders if you need them.

Lesson 126

1. This week you are going to write a fiction piece. Choose what you are going to write: humor? mystery?
2. Today in your workbook write a title; list of characters and their descriptions; and a basic outline of the beginning, middle, and end. For some creative inspiration, here's the opening of a piece called "The Food War."

Simon Wilken was snacking down on a plum with great gusto. He kept a heavy supply of them in his room. Some of the plums he ate weren't finished; they littered the carpet under his king size bed. Simon's favorite fruit and vegetables were part of his everyday life. His parents thought good nutrition was important so they owned a fruit & vegetable store and literally stuffed their son until he'd burst.

When Simon went with his family to their cabin, the pantry back at home came to life. Bananas formed a crude ladder to the floor. Grapes tumbled down to form a cushion. The pineapple almost made a dent in the floor as he came down. Quickly as they fell, the oranges and apples scrambled into a cupboard and came out with scissors. The raisins didn't stay long in that suffocating bag. The brave and gallant colonel mango led the procession into the kitchen while the kiwis defended the rear.

(from https://www.ttms.org/PDFs/03%20Writing%20Samples%20v001%20(Full).pdf)

Lesson 127
1. Write your story.
2. Bring your characters to life with descriptions. Use those adjectives.

Lesson 128
1. Write/edit your story.
2. Make sure you use great words and a variety of different kinds of sentences.

Lesson 129
1. Change one verb and one adjective in your story to make it more descriptive. You could use a thesaurus.
2. Take two sentences and make them one. Do it again.

Lesson 130
1. Read your story out loud and mark any places where you stumbled. Fix those places.
2. Finish editing your story for spelling, capitalization, punctuation…
3. Publish it!
4. Save this in your portfolio.

Lesson 131
1. You are going to be writing paragraphs for the next ten days. There are no worksheets for these. I didn't want to just fill the book with blank lines for writing. If you are able, you could type these.
2. Choose topics from what you have read or from what you have studied for history or science or even music or art or any subject that interests you.
3. The first sentence of your paragraph should be interesting and tell your topic.
4. The middle sentences should give facts, details about the topic.
5. The last sentence should restate the topic and give an opinion about it or tell why it is an interesting/important topic.
6. Write a paragraph as described above.

Lesson 132

1. Write a paragraph.
2. The first sentence of your paragraph should be interesting and tell your topic. Easy ways to gain interest are to ask a question or use a startling fact.
3. The middle sentences should give facts, details about the topic.
4. The last sentence should restate the topic and give an opinion about it or tell why it is an interesting/important topic.

Lesson 133

1. Write a paragraph.
2. The first sentence of your paragraph should be interesting and tell your topic.
3. The middle sentences should give facts, details about the topic.
4. The last sentence should restate the topic and give an opinion about it or tell why it is an interesting/important topic.

Lesson 134

1. Write a paragraph.
2. The first sentence of your paragraph should be interesting and tell your topic.
3. The middle sentences should give facts, details about the topic.
4. The last sentence should restate the topic and give an opinion about it or tell why it is an interesting/important topic.

Lesson 135

1. Write a paragraph.
2. The first sentence of your paragraph should be interesting and tell your topic.
3. The middle sentences should give facts, details about the topic.
4. The last sentence should restate the topic and give an opinion about it or tell why it is an interesting/important topic.

Lesson 136

1. Write a paragraph as usual.
2. The first sentence of your paragraph should be interesting and tell your topic.
3. The middle sentences should give facts, details about the topic.
4. The last sentence should restate the topic and give an opinion about it or tell why it is an interesting/important topic.

Lesson 137

1. Write a paragraph as usual.
2. The first sentence of your paragraph should be interesting and tell your topic.
3. The middle sentences should give facts, details about the topic.
4. The last sentence should restate the topic and give an opinion about it or tell why it is an interesting/important topic.

Lesson 138

1. Write a paragraph as usual.
2. The first sentence of your paragraph should be interesting and tell your topic.

3. The middle sentences should give facts, details about the topic.
4. The last sentence should restate the topic and give an opinion about it or tell why it is an interesting/important topic.

Lesson 139
1. Write a paragraph as usual.
2. The first sentence of your paragraph should be interesting and tell your topic.
3. The middle sentences should give facts, details about the topic.
4. The last sentence should restate the topic and give an opinion about it or tell why it is an interesting/important topic.

Lesson 140
1. Write a paragraph as usual.
2. The first sentence of your paragraph should be interesting and tell your topic.
3. The middle sentences should give facts, details about the topic.
4. The last sentence should restate the topic and give an opinion about it or tell why it is an interesting/important topic.

Lesson 141
1. You lie yourself down. You lay something else down, like a piece of paper. That's tricky enough, but it gets more confusing because lay is the past tense of lie. I lay here just yesterday. If I lied here yesterday, then I was fibbing!
2. Work on the activities in your workbook and learn from your mistakes.

Lesson 142
1. We're working on more tricky words today in your workbook.
2. Good vs. Well
   - Good is an adjective and describes nouns.
   - Well is an adverb.
3. How about your vs. you're?
   - You're is a contraction. It is short for you are.
4. Here are some more clues.
   - When you adapt to something, you change.
   - When you allude to something, you make a reference to it.
   - A site is a location.
5. Try the activity in the workbook and learn from your mistakes. Every mistake is a learning opportunity. Don't waste your opportunities!

Lesson 143
1. In your workbook is another set of confusing words.
2. Affect/Effect
   - Affect is a verb that means something is causing a change.
   - Effect is a noun that means the change caused.
   - I remember which is which by saying, "Cause and **Effect**," to remember that effect is the noun.
     - (Note: There is a verb form of effect, but that's not the common usage.)

3. Its/It's
   - "It's" is a contraction that means it is.
4. Can/May
   - Can means you are physically able.
   - May means you have permission.

Lesson 144

1. In your workbook today, you'll be identifying dependent clauses, the ones that can't stand alone as their own sentences.
2. Then you'll be combining sentences into longer sentences. See if you can do it without using a conjunction. Think about how you could make a better sentence.

Lesson 145

1. Sentence fragments are dependent clauses with no independent clause attached to it. They are not supposed to stand alone. They are just parts, fragments, of a real sentence. Here are some examples.
   - Because I did.
   - And friendly as can be.
   - If you say so.
   - Before he comes in all muddy.
2. Find the fragments. Even though we may speak in fragments sometimes, they aren't properly written that way. Think about dependent clauses. A dependent clause isn't meant to stand alone.

Lesson 146

1. Find the fragments in your workbook today.
2. They are hidden in paragraphs this time. Think about dependent clauses. Those are the key to sentence fragments.

Lesson 147

1. In your workbook there is a spelling activity. Cross out each word part as you use it.
2. If you can't get one, skip it and come back to it because each piece of word is only used once.

Lesson 148

1. Complete your workbook page. Find the fragments in the paragraphs again today.
2. Do you remember what you are looking for?

Lesson 149

1. Write a paragraph. Use great words and check your punctuation and such. There is a workbook page for this.
   - The first sentence of your paragraph should be interesting and tell your topic. Easy ways to gain interest are to ask a question or use a startling fact.
   - The middle sentences should give facts, details about the topic.

- The last sentence should restate the topic and give an opinion about it or tell why it is an interesting/important topic.
- You could save this for your portfolio.

Lesson 150

1. On your workbook page write a short story with no fragments, or write a poem only using fragments.
2. Don't mix and match! Use all fragments or no fragments.

Lesson 151

1. Write a paragraph. Use great words and check your punctuation and such. There is a workbook page for this.
    1. The first sentence of your paragraph should be interesting and tell your topic. Easy ways to gain interest are to ask a question or use a startling fact.
    2. The middle sentences should give facts, details about the topic.
    3. The last sentence should restate the topic and give an opinion about it or tell why it is an interesting/important topic.

Lesson 152

1. Complete the comma exercise in your workbook.
2. Do you want a refresher first? You can turn to Lesson 54 (and Lesson 31).

Lesson 153

1. Correct the punctuation on the worksheet. Look especially for where commas should go, but be on the lookout for missing quotation marks and hyphens.
2. On the second part of your workbook page, you will fill in the apostrophes ('s).

Lesson 154

1. On your worksheet page, you'll be identifying parts of speech. You can review with Lesson 8 if you need to.
2. Remember that words can be used as more than one part of speech, so it is important to look at how it is used in a sentence.
    - I can <u>fly</u>. (verb)
    - It's a <u>fly</u>. (noun)

Lesson 155

1. Read the example of a five-paragraph essay.
2. You'll be writing your own five-paragraph essay. Start thinking about what you'd like to write about. You'll pick your topic in lesson 156.

(introduction) Have you ever wondered what it would be like to float around in space? It's fun to watch videos of astronauts in the space shuttle with their hair sticking up and all their things floating around. What would happen if that was what earth was like? (thesis statement) I think earth without gravity would be an impossible place to live.

(body: main idea 1) Gravity gives us the ability to get around. (details) While we could get around with jet packs, which might be fun for a while, that's only a very limited solution for getting around. We'd have to refuel all the time. If we ran out, we could float away, never to be heard from again. (conclusion) Gravity is what keeps us on earth and lets us do the simplest things like walk from here to there.

(transition) Besides getting around, (main idea 2) gravity lets us play our favorite games. (details) Kicking a soccer ball in no gravity would only result in a lost ball. No one could pitch a baseball in zero gravity; the ball would never reach home plate. A game of chess or checkers could work with Velcro pieces and board I guess, but you'd have to sit strapped in to play! (conclusion) The games that we know just can't be played the same way without gravity.

(transition) Maybe even harder (main idea 3) would be trying to eat without gravity. (details) How could you cut up food? You couldn't. French fries? No way! They would have to make dispensers that only let out one at a time. Of course, the ketchup would float right off and up, up and away. Soup would be a wet mess on the ceiling. We'd have to have lids with fat straws on our bowls and then try to keep the soup from floating out through the straw opening!

(conclusion) Eating a meal without gravity would not be a relaxed and pleasurable affair. (conclusion: restate the thesis) A normal life without gravity is impossible. (sum up and let us know why to care) We rely on gravity for everything, even if we don't realize it. It's enough to keep us from floating away, but not so much that we can't jump, throw a ball, or lift food to our mouths. Earth's gravity is a perfect match for our lives.

Lesson 156

1. Choose a topic to write an essay about. You can choose something you are learning about or something you love that you know a lot about.
2. Write a thesis statement, or the big idea your essay will be about. In the example, the thesis was that it would be impossible to live without gravity. There's a spot for this in your workbook.
3. Now decide on three things you will say about your topic. From the example: getting around, playing games, eating.

Lesson 157

1. Your five-paragraph essay will be due in lesson 162. There are no worksheets for these writing days. If you are able, you could type these.
2. Write an introduction paragraph.
   - Start with an interesting, attention grabbing sentence.
   - Include something fascinating or ask a question.
   - Introduce the things you are going to talk about, but this is not the place for your facts and details!
   - The last sentence should state your main idea for your whole topic, the big idea. That's your thesis statement.
3. There should be at least three sentences.

Lesson 158
1. Write the first paragraph for the body of your essay.
   - Your first sentence should be your topic sentence, the main idea for the paragraph. This paragraph will be about one of those three things you decided to talk about in your essay (Lesson 156). Be interesting!
   - Then include details, the facts.
   - Then state your conclusion.
2. Remember that this will transition to your next paragraph.

Lesson 159
1. Write a second paragraph for the body of your essay.
2. Make sure you use a transition word or phrase at the start of the paragraph.

Lesson 160
1. Write a third paragraph for the body of your essay.
2. Make sure you use a transition at the start of the paragraph.

Lesson 161
1. Write your conclusion paragraph.
   - The first sentence should restate your thesis.
   - Tell why the topic is of interest or important.
2. Wrap it up and give it closure. Can you leave the reader feeling or thinking something?

Lesson 162
1. Read your essay out loud. Mark any awkward parts.
2. Fix any problems.
3. Use the guidelines in your workbook to see if there is anything that needs changing.
4. Finalize your essay.
5. Publish it!
6. How do you think you did? Print out the guidelines and fill in a score for each category.
7. You could save this for your portfolio.

Lesson 163
1. **Appositives** rename a noun. They are nouns but can be phrases. Let me give an example to explain.
   - Charity, the girl in the red sweater, is the leader.
   - Charity is a noun, a person.
   - The girl in the red sweater is a noun phrase. That's the appositive. It came along and gave another name for the noun. It's descriptive but not an adjective. Girl is a noun; Charity is a noun.
2. Here are some more examples.
   - Our home, the one with blue shutters, was built in the 70s.
     - Home and the one are the two nouns.
   - Her dog, Buster, is very friendly.
   - Her dog Buster is very friendly.

- Dog and Buster are the two nouns. In this case, there is no noun phrase, just one word.
- The two versions mean two different things.
  - In the first, she has one dog and his name is Buster, but that's not important to know. The important thing is that her dog is friendly.
  - In the second, she has more than one dog, but it is Buster that is friendly. Watch out for the others! It's essential to know that it's Buster who is friendly. There are no commas in this one because the information is necessary to the meaning of the sentence.

3. In your workbook you'll be finding the sentences with commas in the correct place. An appositive has no commas, two commas, or a comma and a period. Those are the only options. Remember that you don't put one comma between a subject and its verb.

Lesson 164

1. There are two little activities in your workbook today. The second is identifying appositives. The first is to write in the correct past tense of the verbs.
2. Check your answers when you are done. If you got any of the verbs wrong, write another verb that has the same type of past tense.

Lesson 165

1. Today in your workbook you will be placing commas. Think about all the rules, and don't forget appositives.
2. The second part of your page has you writing long sentences. You are not to use a comma and conjunction. You are only allowed to use one independent clause.

Lesson 166

1. You are going to start your end-of-the-year project. Today's assignment is to choose a topic. There's no workbook page for today.
   - If you use EP for science and history, you should read your assignments to see if you have an end-of-the-year project for those subjects that can be combined with this report.
2. There are Research Report Note Taker pages in your workbook. You will use these sheets to record your resources, where you got your information from, and what you learned.
   - For your resources list the titles, authors, and dates of publication. This is true for books or websites.
     - Record whatever information you can find and don't worry about what you can't find, for instance if the website doesn't list an author or the date it was published.
   - The info lines are short. Don't try to copy a sentence. Just write bits to remind you like, *made in 1902*, or *Teddy Roosevelt*.
   - This will help you not copy what others wrote.

3. As you work on your project, remember everything you've learned about writing.
   - You will want an interesting opening to grab their attention.
   - You will want a strong conclusion that will make them think or feel.
   - You will want transitions that move the reader smoothly from paragraph to paragraph in an orderly fashion.

Lesson 167
1. Work on your research. Make sure it's all going on your note taking sheets. Fill in three resources today.
2. List the titles, authors, and dates of publication.

Lesson 168
1. Work on your research. Fill in three resources today.
2. While you are researching, look for someone to quote. Find something someone said that is interesting to use in your report. Copy it down exactly and make sure you write down exactly where you got it from. Include a page number if there is one.

Lesson 169
1. Work on your research.
2. Fill in three resources today.

Lesson 170
1. Today, write your introduction. There aren't any worksheets for these writing days. I suggest you type this if you are able as you'll be working on it over several days.
2. The *last sentence* is going to be your main idea. It will tell the main idea of your research report. It should be as specific as is possible.
3. Your first sentence should be interesting. It should make people want to read your biography. An easy way to get people interested is asking them a question. Other ways include using a quote or by making an interesting observation.
4. A research report will be longer than a five-paragraph essay. It is the same, however, in having an introduction, supporting details, and a conclusion.
   - You'll want to catch your reader's attention with your opening.
   - You'll need a clear thesis that points to what you will be discussing.
   - Multiple paragraphs can be about the same point. Each paragraph, though, should have a topic sentence and details.
   - Use facts, statistics, examples, and quotes. Don't just tell your information, show it.
   - Use a formal voice. Sound professional.
   - Use transition words and phrases that guide the reader from one topic to another, connecting the paragraphs.
   - Put your information in a logical order.
   - Don't forget to use long and varied sentences.
   - Your conclusion should sum up and restate the thesis.

Lesson 171

1. Today you are going to organize. Think about your introduction. What is your thesis? What is the point you are going to make with your research report? You need to use your facts to make that point.

2. Gather your facts into groups. All of the facts in each group should be about one topic. The goal would be to have at least nine groups of two or three facts. Try to use the facts you have and see how they relate to each other. Find more facts if you need to.

3. Color code them. Mark the ones that go together all the same color. Then make a key on today's workbook page by writing the name of the topic and coloring in the box next to it with the color you used to mark the facts that support that topic. (Save the first box for numbering.)

4. Now you are going to decide the order that you are going to use your groups. Each group will be one paragraph. Think about how your topics will flow in your report. One has to lead to the next.

5. If you have any group with four or more facts, think about if it should be divided into two separate groups.

6. Decide on their order and number your key by writing numbers in the first box of each line.

   - An example of topics for Genghis Khan might be:
     - childhood
     - leader
       - growing power, merit based, taking charge
     - military leader
       - raids, strategy, invention
     - end of life
     - legacy
   - Each could be a paragraph. "Leader" and "military leader" could be paragraphs introducing that section of the report and then three paragraphs following supporting it, each like a mini essay in the report.

Lesson 172

1. Make sure your facts are organized, not just a list of information you want to get out. For instance, you could have several paragraphs about the building of the Panama Canal and several paragraphs about its use and impact.

2. When you are happy with your order, write it down. You will use the outline form in your workbook to write your information.
   - You may decide that some of your topics should be combined. You may decide that some of the topics don't fit into your thesis and overall theme and not use them at all.

3. You have already written your intro. For your outline, you are just going to be working on the body of your report.

4. Each line is for a topic of a paragraph. The goal is to have *at least* five but hopefully nine.

5. Write a topic. Then write in the facts that go with it. Think about what a good order would be to put them in. Don't just write them in the order you found them.

6. There are three pages in the workbook for this.

Lesson 173

1. Today start with your first topic on your outline and begin writing. Remember that the first sentence of your paragraph gives the main idea for that paragraph. Each paragraph has a topic sentence, the details that tell about that idea, and a conclusion sentence. You don't need strong conclusion sentences for every paragraph. Use your first and last sentences as transitions to close a topic and link it to the next.
2. You need to write three paragraphs today unless you intend on writing a really long report. Once, in seventh grade, I wrote a report that was 27 pages long! (It did have some pictures and diagrams, though.)

Lesson 174

1. Write at least three more paragraphs. Make sure they are written in the right format.
2. Also, think about how to transition from one paragraph to another. Remember transition words?

Lesson 175

1. Write another three paragraphs today. Try to finish all of your topic paragraphs listed on your outline. Don't forget to use your quote and to use it in quotations marks. Make sure you add in who said it.
2. Are you giving examples, facts, and details in each paragraph to support your topic sentence?
   - Add factual power to your paragraph with facts, statistics, reasons, anecdotes, quotes, examples, steps, results, and details (including sight, sound, smell, and feel).
3. Don't forget to use your quote and to use it in quotations marks. Make sure you know where you got it from.

Lesson 176

1. Write your conclusion.
2. The first sentence of your conclusion retells your "thesis" or main idea of your report.
   - Don't use the same exact sentence from the introduction!
3. You need to add another sentence and then conclude with a final sentence.
4. Your final sentence should give meaning to your report.
   - Maybe use the word "I" and tell what you think of the whole thing, why it is important.

Lesson 177

1. Use the editing guide in your workbook.
2. Judge your report. Where do you need to do some work to make it better?
3. Make it better.
4. Add similes, descriptions, more interesting word choices.
5. Make sure you have long and short sentences. Think about how you practiced with long sentences.

Lesson 178
1. Read your report out loud. Mark anywhere that you stumbled while reading.
2. Fix all the problems. Anything that made you stumble, reword.
3. Look at capitalization, commas, and sentence structure.
4. Now you are going to add something. Right after your quote you need to tell the reader where the quote is from. After the quote write the author's last name and the page number like this. (author, number) If there is no page number, just list the author. If there is no author, put the webpage name. Tomorrow you are going to make a list of the resources you used, and the reader will be able to use what you write by your quote to find what resource it was from. If the quote is something someone said, you need to have in your report who said it. The parenthesis is for where you found it, not who said it.

Lesson 179
1. Today make sure your report is the way you like it. Add a title or a title page.
2. Finally, you are going to add a **bibliography**, a list of all the resources you used to get your information.
3. Make a page with the title, *Bibliography*.
4. Write out your resources in an alphabetical list on that page. Here is how you could list things in your bibliography.
   - Last, First M. *Book Title*. City of Publication: Publisher, Year Published. Year Printed.
   - Last, First M. "Article Title."*Website Title*. Website Publisher, Date on article. Date (month/year) you read it.
   - You can leave out any information that you don't have. Do your best.

Lesson 180
1. Publish and present!
2. Have your readers give you feedback in your workbook.

EP Language Arts 6

Workbook Answers

Lesson 2

Spelling corrections are bold, punctuation marks are circled, and capitalization errors are underlined.

<u>booker</u> to <u>washington</u> was a great **educator** of <u>african</u> <u>americans</u> in the late 1800s and early 1900s. **founding** **thousands** of schools throughout the <u>south</u>, he knew that education was highly important for the social advancement of his race. He was also a political advisor to both FDR and <u>president</u> <u>taft</u>, and greatly improved the **racial** relations in <u>america</u> during his lifetime.

A B C D E F G H I J K L M N O P Q R S T U V W X Y Z

R A C C O O N

A B C D E F G H I J K L M N O P Q R S T U V W X Y Z

K A N G A R O O

Lesson 3

A gold/wing moth is be/tween the scis/sors and the ink bot/tle on the desk.

Last night it flew hun/dreds of cir/cles a/round a glass bulb and a flame wire.

The wings are a soft gold; it is the gold of il/lu/mi/nat/ed in/i/tials in man/u/scripts of the me/di/e/val monks.

(Note: medieval might trip some up; most pronounce it in 3 syllables me-die-val. The goal is understanding syllables. It's okay if that one is marked as it's pronounced in your home.)

collect	because
consider	aghast
sensational	agony
trouble	cereal
existence	photosynthesis

Lesson 4

Spelling corrections are bold, punctuation marks are circled, and capitalization errors are underlined.

<u>charles</u> <u>lindbergh</u> was **fascinated** with flying. <u>though</u> trained as a **mechanical** engineer, he is best known for being the first person to fly across the <u>atlantic</u>. He did this in 1927, not even twenty-five years after the <u>wright</u> **brothers'** first flight in 1903.

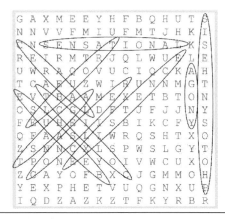

Lesson 6

Spelling corrections are bold, punctuation marks are circled, and capitalization errors are underlined.

Gus Grissom was a **pioneer** of <u>american</u> space exploration. He was one of the original Mercury Seven, and he was the **second** <u>american</u> ever to go to space.

Born in 1926 in Mitchell, Indiana, Grissom was originally a combat pilot in the <u>korean</u> <u>war</u>. He moved on to be an Air Force test pilot, and finally a NASA **astronaut**. He made his first journey into space in 1961 aboard the Liberty Bell 7. In the year 1965, he became the first man in history to make a return trip to space as he **journeyed** aboard the Gemini 3. During preparations for his third trip to space, Gus Grissom died in a fire during a launch pad test for Apollo 1.

Before his death, Grissom said the following: "If we die, we want people to **accept** it. We're in a risky **business**, and we hope that if anything happens to us it will not delay the program. The **conquest** of space is worth the risk of life."

Lesson 8

Lesson 8: Parts of Speech
Language Arts 6

Circle the part of speech that correctly labels the underlined word in each sentence.

Dancing is my <u>favorite</u> activity. noun adverb (adjective)

Did that door just shut <u>itself</u>? verb (pronoun) adverb

The concert <u>was</u> fabulous. (verb) preposition noun

The morning <u>swim</u> was cold. (noun) verb adjective

Whose shoes are <u>by</u> the door? adverb verb (preposition)

Let's go to the library <u>soon</u>. noun (adverb) pronoun

<u>Chicago</u> gets many visitors. verb (noun) adjective

She looked <u>very</u> pretty. adjective pronoun (adverb)

That was a <u>costly</u> mistake. adverb verb (adjective)

Please help <u>yourself</u> to the fridge. noun (pronoun) verb

The storm raged <u>during</u> the night. (preposition) verb noun

Can you <u>chop</u> the vegetables? (verb) noun adjective

<u>Yesterday</u> was my birthday. verb pronoun (adverb)

Lesson 9

Lesson 9: Grammar Review
Language Arts 6

Of the bolded words, circle the one that matches the part of speech to the side of the sentence

Did you look **(through)** the mail yet? Preposition

I hope to go for a **(jog)** first thing tomorrow. Noun

Her **(curly)** hair is fun to play with. Adjective

I can't get all of this done by **(myself)** Pronoun

Her **(exquisitely)** designed cake won first prize. Adverb

God's love **(is)** amazing. Verb

Head **(toward)** the gas station and turn right. Preposition

Are you up for a **(leisurely)** stroll? Adjective

I have a hair appointment **(tomorrow)** morning. Adverb

What do you **(think)** about the proposal? Verb

How can **(you)** stand to eat fish? Pronoun

His **(bravery)** was astounding. Noun

Lesson 10

Lesson 10: Combining Sentences
Language Arts 6

(Answers will vary. Suggestions given.)

Louisa May Alcott, a homeschooler with a passion for reading, wrote over 30 books with *Little Women* being the most famous.

Mexican-born Octabiano Larrazolo, the first Hispanic U.S. senator, represented New Mexico where he had previously served as governor.

The oldest known pair of ice skates, dating back to 3000 B.C., were found at the bottom of a lake in Switzerland, and were made from a large animal's leg bone.

Lesson 11

Day 11: Metaphors
Language Arts 6

Answer the following questions as a refresher course on metaphors.

We could have people over more often if the *house wasn't such a pigsty*.

This metaphor compares the house to a pigsty because...
- a. ...we raise pigs.
- b. ...it stinks like a barn.
- (c.) ...it is messy.

I woke up to a *blanket of snow* on the ground.

This metaphor compares the snow to a blanket because...
- (a.) ...it covered the ground.
- b. ...it was warm.
- c. ...it was on the bed.

Emma's legs were Jell-O as she took her place on the stage.

This metaphor compares Emma's legs to Jell-O because...
- a. ...she spilled her snack on them.
- (b.) ...they were shaking from her nerves.
- c. ...she was hungry.

Sam, *the family early bird*, got the rest of the cereal.

This metaphor compares Sam to an early bird because...
- a. ...he liked worms.
- (b.) ...he got up before everyone else.
- c. ...he enjoyed singing in the morning.

Lesson 13

Can you unscramble the letters to correctly spell a word to fit the blank? If you need help, have someone read you the unscrambled words from the answer key and then you can try to spell them correctly.

The ORUMSONE spider made me jump.

enormous

We called an IAELICNETRC to fix our fuse.

electrician

Being able to keep clean continued to UEELD him.

elude

You have a worried IEPNXEORSS on your face.

expression

Riding a roller coaster fills me with XHOLRATIAENI.

exhilaration

Water is IANTSSEEL for life.

essential

That pianist's talent was RROEATDNAXIYR!

extraordinary

Last night's sunset was absolutely UTQISEIXE.

exquisite

The project NNGEIREE laid out the plans for the bridge.

engineer

I cannot contain my ITXMECNETE about our vacation!

excitement

Lesson 14

Turn the sentence fragments into complete sentences. (Answers will vary.)

The big, scary dog.

_____

Watched the gorgeous sunset.

_____

Her long, curly hair.

_____

Ran down the road.

_____

Across the street.

_____

Select the option that correctly fills in each blank.

They expected _____ to do all of their laundry.

Mom and I   (Mom and me)

There was _____ much laundry for us to do it all.

to   two   (too)

_____ did get all of the clean laundry folded, though.

(Mom and I)   Mom and me

_____ fortunate we were willing to help at all!

Their   There   (They're)

Lesson 15

Put an X on the line if the sentence is a simile, and leave it blank if it's not. Then write a simile containing an animal on the lines.

My mom calls me a couch potato.   _____

The pillows were fluffy clouds.   _____

My brother eats like a pig.   X

She's as light as a feather.   X

He was drowning in a sea of grief.   _____

My coach was an ogre when we lost.   _____

The car was like a rocket.   X

The book was good food for thought.   _____

Her stomach was flipping like a gymnast.   X

Go left at the fork in the road.   _____

She was as happy as a clam.   X

They tiptoed like ballerinas.   X

The promise was a steady rock.   _____

Her eyes burned like a campfire.   X

The betrayal was a knife in the back.   _____

_____

_____

Lesson 18

Put the correct present tense of the verb in parenthesis into the blank. Make sure to figure out what the subject of the sentence is, and then match the verb to it.

Everyone at the game, including the umpires, **hopes** that the rain lets up soon. (to hope)

The nights **are** long, but the days **are** short. (to be)

This bread **tastes** stale to me. (to taste)

My mom, with the help of my dad, **has** mastered the new Lego video game. (to have)

The twelve gallons of milk for the after-play snack **make** it difficult to fit anything else in the fridge. (to make)

The young girl **knows** her math facts but has trouble recalling them quickly. (to know)

The finish on our hardwood floors **needs** to be replaced due to scratches. (to need)

Each of the children **comes** to the park hoping for a free swing. (to come)

The producers of the show **announce** the upcoming musical schedule at the end of the show. (to announce)

The audience **gasps** at the scary parts of the film. (to gasp)

The airplane **flies** to the destination at a brisk pace. (to fly)

Lesson 19

Fill in the blanks of the story while someone reads it to you from the answer key. Do the best you can to spell them correctly.

___Everything___ about the ___continent___ of

Europe ___appealed___ to Mandy. She loved the old

___architecture___ and the beautiful ___scenery___.

Travelling on an ___airplane___ for hours to get there

even sounded fun! She was antsy with ___anticipation___

to take a trip there. Unfortunately, due to the large

___expense___ of such a trip, she would have to be

___patient___ and save her money for a ___while___.

Lesson 20

Match the simile beginning with the ending that makes the most sense. Write the letter of the ending in the blank beside the beginning.

Beginning		Ending	
As hungry as	h	a.	nails
As flat as	c	b.	a bee
As solid as	i	c.	a pancake
As quiet as	d	d.	a mouse
As busy as	b	e.	a bat
As cold as	k	f.	dirt
As good as	l	g.	the hills
As blind as	e	h.	a wolf
As tough as	a	i.	a rock
As easy as	m	j.	silk
As poor as	f	k.	ice
As old as	g	l.	gold
As smooth as	j	m.	pie

Lesson 23

Choose the selection that corrects any error that might exist in the underlined portions of the paragraphs. If there is no error, select "no change."

Janine reached into her <u>bag, hoping</u> to find her appointment card. She <u>couldn't remember</u> what time she was supposed to arrive at the dentist. When she finally found <u>it, she</u> realized she had the wrong day!
a. bag hoping
b. couldn't, remember
c. it she
(d.) **no change**

Luke opened all of his birthday <u>gifts at</u> a frazzled pace. He was hoping to receive the gift he wanted the <u>most a</u> painting from his grandfather. When he opened the last <u>box, his</u> eyes teared up as he saw a portrait of himself staring back at him. His grandfather had an incredible talent.
a. gifts, at
(b.) **most, a**
c. box his
d. no change

The president of the United <u>States has</u> a tough job. He often has to put his own convictions <u>aside for</u> the good of the country. Any time there's a national <u>problem everyone</u> blames the president. I wouldn't want that job.
a. States, has
b. aside, for
(c.) **problem, everyone**
d. no change

Lesson 24

Fix the fragments! Choose the selection that corrects any error that might exist in the underlined portions of the paragraphs. If there is no error, select "no change."

The twisty mountain roads made Jordan feel queasy. He loved <u>reading, but</u> he decided it would be smart to put his book <u>down until</u> the roads were straight again. Putting the book <u>down and looking</u> out the window helped him feel better. As a bonus, he got to enjoy the mountain beauty!
a. reading but
b. down. Until
c. down, looking
(d.) **no change**

The essay assignment loomed in front of Andrew. He freely <u>admitted. Writing</u> didn't come easily to him, so he always put writing assignments off until the last minute. His mom gently pointed out that if he'd do them a little bit at a <u>time, they'd</u> be much easier to complete. He knew she was <u>right, and</u> he decided to buckle down and get to work.
(a.) **admitted writing**
b. time. They'd
c. right. And
d. no change

The Statue of Liberty has been a welcome sight for many immigrants across the years. As they arrived at nearby Ellis <u>Island, they</u> would see the statue and know they were entering a land of freedom and <u>democracy. Standing</u> over 151 feet <u>tall. It</u> is a quintessential emblem of liberty, known throughout the world.
a. Island. They
b. democracy, standing
(c.) **tall, it**
d. no change

Lesson 25

Spelling corrections are bold, punctuation marks are circled.

When you put a piece of food into your mouth(,) **digestion** begins. As you **chew** your food(,) saliva helps break it down further. Once you swallow(,) food **travels** through your esophagus and enters your **stomach** where **digestive** juices break it down even more. From the **stomach**(,) food **travels farther** into the small **intestine** where nutrients are absorbed. What is left enters the large **intestine** where water is absorbed and waste is stored(.)(⸮)

Can you hand me all of the (knife) __knives__ ?

Those (person) __people__ aren't being very quiet in the library.

There must have been eight (deer) __deer__ on that hill!

My aunt's house has a problem with (mouse) __mice__ .

The (mosquito) __mosquitoes__ are out in full force this evening.

The school had a wide variety for our (lunch) __lunches__ .

Lesson 26

Spelling corrections are bold, punctuation marks are circled, and capitalization errors are underlined.

Synonyms are words with **similar** meanings(.) **antonyms**(,) on the other hand(,) are words with opposite meanings. For instance(,) cold and hot are **antonyms**(,) but <u>Cold</u> and chilly are synonyms. A good way to remember them is to think that synonym sounds a little like **similar**(,) and if you're anti-something, you're opposed to it. Can you think of examples of synonyms and **antonyms**(?)

theory	__theories__	alga	__algae__
shelf	__shelves__	stimulus	__stimuli__
piano	__pianos__	index	__indices__
cliff	__cliffs__	thesis	__theses__
hitch	__hitches__	medium	__media__
hero	__heroes__	series	__series__

Lesson 28

Spell these words as they are read to you from the Lesson Guide. Do your best and review any mistakes you make.

advice	advise
distress	dissipate
thorough	through
lose	loose
coordinate	cooperate
disastrous	disciple
groceries	businesses
dominoes	temperature
yourselves	xylophone

Lesson 33

For each of the following, choose the sentence that has the correct comma usage.

(a.) You are, I'm certain, going to be great!

(c.) Penelope and Jason each brought milk to the breakfast.

(b.) I'm speaking, Sarah, so I'd like you to be quiet.

(a.) Please get your shoes, jacket, and scarf off the living room floor.

(c.) My mom, Gail, is the one you're looking for.

(a.) Though the storm lasted all night, I slept like a baby.

Lesson 36

Lesson 36: Simple, Compound, or Complex — Language Arts 6

For each of the following sentences, select which type of sentence is used.

Your bedroom smells like dirty laundry.
(**simple**)   compound   complex

Although I wash your clothes, you should put them in the hamper yourself.
simple   compound   (**complex**)

I see dirty socks under your bed, and I see a towel wadded up in the corner.
simple   (**compound**)   complex

Could you please get it all to the laundry room?
(**simple**)   compound   complex

I'm about to start a load anyway, and I'd like for your stuff to be included.
simple   (**compound**)   complex

You'll notice an immediate difference in your room.
(**simple**)   compound   complex

Besides smelling fresher, your room will be cleaner, too.
simple   compound   (**complex**)

Lesson 38

Lesson 38: Spelling — Language Arts 6

Fill in the blanks of the story as someone reads it to you from the answer key.

I asked my mom for some __advice__ about an

upcoming babysitting job. I was nervous because it was

my first one with a preschooler. As she put away the

__groceries__, she chose to __advise__ me

about keeping him occupied. "Try __dominoes__,"

she suggested, "or even make music with your old

__xylophone__." I could feel my __distress__

begin to __dissipate__ at her great suggestions.

Lesson 39

Lesson 39: Combining Sentences — Language Arts 6

(Answers will vary. Suggestions given.)

Albert Einstein, who often daydreamed in class during school because so many ideas filled his mind, went on to graduate with a degree in physics and is probably the most famous physicist of the 20th century.

Einstein is most famous for his theory of relativity, which asserts that E equals mc squared, or energy equals mass times the speed of light squared.

Lesson 40

Lesson 40: Commas — Language Arts 6

Choose the selection that corrects any error that might exist in the underlined portions of the sentences. If there is no error, select "no change."

The drink selections for the evening are, Dr Pepper, Diet Coke, Sprite, water, or iced tea.
a. selections, for
(**b.**) **are Dr**
c. water; or
d. no change

Thank you, Sandra, for taking the time, however brief, to explain the diagram to us.
a. you Sandra
b. time however
c. brief to
(**d.**) **no change**

The wind blew swiftly, across the yard, picking up leaves and swirling them around until they landed, ready to be picked up again.
(**a.**) **swiftly across**
b. yard picking
c. landed ready
d. no change

The leash jingled as I picked it up, signaling to my dog that it was time to take our evening walk his favorite activity.
a. jingled, as
b. up signaling
(**c.**) **walk, his**
d. no change

Lesson 41

Fill in the missing letter for the words below. Some are easy, some are hard!

s **i** eve	loo **s** e	Feb **r** uary
lett **u** ce	spe **c** ial	sle **e** ve
absen **c** e	def **i** nite	adverti **s** e
crit **i** cize	m **y** sterious	**o** fficial
hum **o** rous	camo **u** flage	med **i** cine
presen **c** e	tom **o** rrow	spe **e** ch
para **c** hute	comp **e** tition	su **r** prise
We **d** nesday	w **h** ether	ans **w** er
stren **g** th	sold **i** er	resta **u** rant
suppose **d** ly	pr **e** fer	recogni **z** e
li **c** ense	interf **e** re	ju **d** gment
gover **n** ment	independ **e** nce	exist **e** nce
desp **e** rate	def **i** nitely	basic **a** lly

Lesson 42

(Answers will vary. Suggestions given.)

In the 1400s, Johan Guttenberg invented the printing press, which used movable metal letters making printing much quicker.

Before the invention of the printing press, printing was painstakingly done by hand, using materials such as clay, papyrus, wax, and parchment.

After the printing press, knowledge could spread as quickly as books could be printed, which caused an eruption of innovation we know as the Renaissance.

Lesson 44

How many independent clauses are in the following sentences? Answer the questions about each sentence.

My mom told me to take the dog outside and do my chores before I watched a movie.
- ○ There are no independent clauses.
- ● This sentence has one independent clause.
- ○ This sentence has two independent clauses.

My mom was worried **that I would forget to do my work.**
- ○ The bold part of the sentence is the independent clause.
- ● The non-bold part of the sentence is the independent clause.
- ○ This sentence has no independent clause.

I tend to rush my work sometimes; I really love watching movies.
- ○ There are no independent clauses.
- ○ This sentence has one independent clause.
- ● This sentence has two independent clauses.

My favorite movie, **one based on a book,** has a lot of great actors.
- ○ The bold part of the sentence is an independent clause.
- ● The bold part of the sentence is not an independent clause.
- ○ This sentence has two independent clauses.

That I can't watch a movie without doing my work.
- ● There are no independent clauses.
- ○ This sentence has one independent clause.
- ○ This sentence has two independent clauses.

Lesson 51

Properly punctuate the dialogue at the top of the page. Then use the lines at the bottom of the page to copy the interesting quote by your historical person.

"Come here," he said.

She got up and crossed the room. "What is it?"

"A geode."

She asked again, "And that is what exactly?"

He brought out a hammer. "Watch and see."

Quote:_____

_____

_____

_____

Author: _____

Date written: _____

Source: _____

_____

Lesson 57

I used to ride bikes, skip rope, run races, and roll in the grass.

Now I cook and clean, and my kids do all those things.

When I was young, I thought being old would be fun.

Now that I'm old, as if thirty-seven is old, I think I was right.

I have a bunch of fun, energetic, creative kids.

"It's tomorrow," my son says in the mornings.

We try and explain that it's today, not tomorrow.

He'll jump up and say, "Let's eat, Mom!"

We haven't lived near Philadelphia, Pennsylvania, since May 31, 2002.

Riding a bike is something you never forget how to do.

Lesson 59

Select which sentence type describes the sentence given.

What a fantastic day!
○ declarative ○ interrogative ● exclamatory ○ imperative

Where do you keep the bandages?
○ declarative ● interrogative ○ exclamatory ○ imperative

My brother is a 6'5" basketball sensation.
● declarative ○ interrogative ○ exclamatory ○ imperative

Please stop screaming.
○ declarative ○ interrogative ○ exclamatory ● imperative

What is all over your shirt?
○ declarative ● interrogative ○ exclamatory ○ imperative

When I was little, I really enjoyed riding my bike.
● declarative ○ interrogative ○ exclamatory ○ imperative

I can't believe she said that!
○ declarative ○ interrogative ● exclamatory ○ imperative

What would you like for lunch?
○ declarative ● interrogative ○ exclamatory ○ imperative

Keep your hands to yourself.
○ declarative ○ interrogative ○ exclamatory ● imperative

It's really hot in here today.
● declarative ○ interrogative ○ exclamatory ○ imperative

Look out! (either answer is correct)
○ declarative ○ interrogative ● exclamatory ● imperative

Lesson 66

Spelling corrections are bold, punctuation marks are circled, and capitalization errors are underlined.

Paper-making has come a long **way** over the centuries. First, trees are harvested and sent to the mill. Next, logs are sent **through** a machine that strips them of **their** bark. Eventually, the pulp is soaked and then pressed together and dried. Automated machines can make huge rolls of thin paper that can be cut into whatever size is needed.

There are three main types of rock. Sedimentary rocks are **made** up of layers of sediment that have compacted together over time. Igneous rocks are formed when magma cools and hardens. Sometimes they form inside the earth's surface. Other times they form on the surface after a volcanic eruption expels them. Metamorphic rocks are rocks that used to be one of the other **two** types and changed **due** to things like weather, heat, and pressure.

Lesson 72

Underline the adjectives in the sentences below. If you need help, try to find the nouns first, and then underline the words that are describing them. There are multiple adjectives in each sentence.

The <u>small</u>, <u>yippy</u> dog barked well into the <u>summer</u> night.

The <u>young</u> mom brought <u>her newborn</u> baby to the doctor.

<u>My helpful</u> brother will happily carry <u>your heavy</u> bags.

Whose <u>striped</u> bag is sitting on the <u>filthy</u> floor?

Stephanie lost <u>her purple</u> ring after <u>three</u> months.

The <u>baby</u> zebra galloped across the <u>dusty</u> terrain.

<u>That</u> dog has <u>beautiful</u> fur.

The <u>colorful</u> graphics made the <u>computer</u> game extra <u>fun</u>.

The <u>popcorn</u> ceiling left <u>white</u> flakes in <u>my</u> hair as I painted it.

<u>My cozy</u> bed is loudly calling <u>my</u> name at the end of <u>this</u> day.

We had a <u>delicious</u> dinner of <u>juicy</u> steak and <u>mashed</u> potatoes.

The <u>quick brown</u> fox jumped over the <u>lazy</u> dog.

The <u>colorful</u> leaves fell to the <u>cold</u> ground in the <u>gentle</u> breeze.

Lesson 74

Lesson 74: Adjective Quiz
Language Arts 6

Answer the following questions about adjectives. Learn from any mistakes!

Which word in this sentence is an adjective?
The doctor gave a prescription to the sickly girl.

(d.) sickly

Which bolded word is not an adjective?

(a.)   I'm **perfectly** capable of cooking dinner.

Which of the choices is the correct form of the superlative for the sentence?
That was the _____ nap I've ever had.

(c.) most peaceful

Which choice correctly completes the sentence?
Your creative ability is _____ than mine.

(d.) better

Which words correctly complete the sentence?
_____ trees _____ really blooming this spring.

(b.) Those... are

What is the correct way to write the proper adjective in the sentence?
The north american continent has a wide array of weather.

(b.) North American

Lesson 76

Lesson 76: Advertising
Language Arts 6

For each example given, write on the line which type of advertising is being demonstrated.

A used car dealership lists a minivan online for $2,999. When you get to the lot, you notice that the cheapest vehicle they have available is $5,999.

bait and switch

A magazine ad for chips speaks of how their bags contain 20% more than "the other guy." (Of course, the ad doesn't mention that their bag also costs 20% more.)

product comparison

A television commercial for a smartphone invites you to "be yourself" and switch to their "unique" phone.

individuality

A radio advertisement for an internet provider implores you to "join the millions of people who have made the switch."

bandwagon

An internet banner ad displays a picture of a popular teen actor flashing his pearly whites while holding a particular brand's tube of whitening toothpaste.

celebrity spokesperson

A full page newspaper ad shows a farmer in overalls standing in front of a truck. An American flag is behind him and the ad touts that the truck is "proudly American made for everyday Americans like you."

glittering generalities/plain folk

Lesson 78

Lesson 78: Advertisement
Language Arts 6

Use the ad at the bottom of the page to answer these questions.
(Answers will vary)

What is the message of the advertisement? **Eating more fruit will help you keep fit; feeding your kids fruit can help them stay healthy.**

What persuasive techniques is the advertisement using? **plain folk, loaded language, emotion**

Who is the target audience of the advertisement? **young parents, people who want to be healthy**

Is the ad effective? Why or why not?

(personal opinion; answers will vary)

Eat More Fruit
and keep fit

Lesson 82

Lesson 82: Parts of Speech
Language Arts 6

Would **you** like **to** go **to** the **store** with me?   Preposition
(a preposition must be part of a prepositional phrase)

Tomorrow is my brother's golden **birthday**.   Noun

The **novel** was so **thick** it **seemed** unending.   Adjective

The **wind** made the door **seem** to shut **itself**.   Pronoun

The **long line** took us **long** into the night.   Adverb

My **sister** **is** the world's **best** ballet **dancer**.   Verb

My green blanket is so cozy.   noun   adverb   (adjective)

Please put it down on the table.   verb   (pronoun)   adverb

I finally watched the program.   (verb)   preposition   noun

Did you take a sip of my drink?   (noun)   verb   adjective

The dog jumped out the window!   adverb verb (preposition)

The church steeple rises high.   noun   (adverb)   pronoun

Lesson 84

Lesson 84: Parts of Speech
Language Arts 6

Circle the part of speech that correctly labels the underlined word in each sentence.

Her manners <u>greatly</u> pleased him.   noun   (adverb)   adjective

Please <u>place</u> it gently on the counter.   (verb)   noun   adverb

The bridge collapsed <u>into</u> the river.   verb   (preposition)   noun

The <u>golden</u> sun crested the horizon.   noun   verb   (adjective)

Her <u>walk</u> was more of a waddle.   verb   (noun)   preposition

The bird bumped <u>its</u> beak on the door.   noun   verb   (pronoun)

Of the bolded words, underline the one that matches the part of speech to the side of the sentence.

We went for a walk **after** dinner.   Preposition

The **softball** didn't feel **soft** when it hit my nose.   Noun

It took a **long** time to **drive** to Milwaukee.   Adjective

I'm not sure Mr. Lawson liked **his** gift.   Pronoun

My **schedule** is clear, so let's get together **soon**.   Adverb

The dog **delighted** the crowd with his tricks.   Verb

Lesson 87

Lesson 87: Homophones
Language Arts 6

Choose the correct homophone to fit the blanks in the sentences.

_____ completely ready to go?
whose   (who's)

The girls needed to clean _____ room before playing.
there   they're   (their)

There's _____ much snow in the forecast for November!
(too)   two   to

Would you like the last _____ of pie?
peace   (piece)

I saw a _____ scamper into the woods.
(doe)   dough

I am _____ explaining this to you.
threw   (through)

I got my hair _____ a darker color last week.
died   (dyed)

My dad spent the weekend fixing our van's _____.
(brakes)   breaks'

My little brother is _____ years old today.
(eight)   ate

Will you help me _____ these books to the garage?
hall   (haul)

Lesson 88

Lesson 88: Subject vs. Object Pronouns
Language Arts 6

Choose the correct pronoun to fill in the blank. If you need help, try to determine if the needed pronoun should be a subject or an object pronoun.

The boys tried to beat _____ at chess.
Rachel and I   (Rachel and me)

Mom is visiting family, so feel free to write _____ and Aunt Carrie a letter.
she   (her)

I saw the one who took your pencil. It was _____, that boy in the blue.
(he)   him

_____ wore matching sweaters to the fair.
Her and I   (She and I)   Her and me

It could have been _____ who raked our yard in kindness.
(he)   him

_____ switch desks almost every day.
(She and Lucy)   Lucy and her

Dad sat between _____ and Jessie so they wouldn't fight.
she   (her)

Matthew realized that neither _____ nor James was ready for the big trip.
(he)   him

Becky asked Iris and Denise to come sit by _____.
she and Lillian   (Lillian and her)

Lesson 89

Lesson 89: Pronouns
Language Arts 6

Choose the correct pronoun to fill in the blank.

My two-year-old insists on getting dressed _____.
(himself)   hisself   his self

_____ look exactly alike.
Her and her father   (She and her father)   Her father and herself

Either _____ or Michelle will pick you up today.
(he)   him   himself

_____ incessant screaming is giving me a headache.
There   Theirs   (Their)

It was _____ who ate all of the chips yesterday.
(she)   her   herself

Can you give the letter to _____ or Jake?
they   (them)   themselves

I wish I was better at basketball than _____.
(he)   him   himself

Since Justin is the messiest one here, I assume the trash on the floor is _____.
(his)   his'   theirs

We found _____ hiding under the desk.
she   (her)   herself

Would you ask _____ if he wants something to drink?
he   (him)   himself

Lesson 90

Lesson 90: Pronouns Language Arts 6

Choose the correct pronoun to fill in the blank.

It was _____ who did the dishes for you.
me   myself   (I)

My mom asked my sister and _____ to clean our room.
(me)   myself   I

Liz and _____ spent the entire day on the computer.
me   myself   (I)

My mom was not happy with _____ rearranging the living room furniture without asking.
me   myself   (my)

Between you and _____, that movie could have been a lot better.
(me)   myself   I

Amy was surprised I spent all night on the phone with _____.
She and Jenna   (Jenna and her)

The ringing cellphone in my pocket gave away _____ hiding spot for hide and seek.
(Jennifer's and my)   Me and Jennifer's   Myself and Jennifer's

Are you upset with _____ choosing of the read aloud?
me   myself   (my)

When it comes to cooking, you know more than _____.
me   mine   (I)

Lesson 91

Lesson 91: Proofreading Language Arts 6

Spelling corrections are bold, punctuation marks are circled, and capitalization errors are underlined.

You're halfway through this course. What kinds of things have you learned this year⊙ You've learned lots of things about commas. For instance⊙ they should go after introductory words in a sentence. You've learned about homophones and are learning **which** ones are **which**. You've done lots of proofreading, spotting **errors** in spelling and grammar throughout many sentences and **paragraphs**. **Your** writing has improved as you've written essays⊙ book reports⊙ short stories⊙ and more. You know that **similes** use like or as and **metaphors** say something is something else. You know better than **I** where a subject pronoun goes and where an object pronoun goes. And the best part of it all is, you are learning from your mistakes. It's okay to get things wrong⊙ **just** keep learning. I wonder what the second half of the **course** will hold.

Lesson 92

Lesson 92: Semicolons Language Arts 6

Insert the semicolons in the correct spots in the sentences below.

It's hot today⊙ therefore, you won't need your jacket.

You should do the dishes⊙ then you can play video games.

My sister is older than me⊙ my brother is younger than me.

Wash your hands first⊙ then you can help me cook.

Let's go to Frosty's⊙ they have good pizza.

Something is flashing in the sky⊙ perhaps it's an airplane.

This is a good book⊙ someone worked hard on it.

I enjoy writing⊙ math, on the other hand, is hard for me.

You wash the car⊙ I'll vacuum it out.

We don't have cable⊙ we prefer to watch movies on DVD.

Your room is a mess⊙ you should clean it immediately.

Please leave your shoes outside⊙ I just had the carpets cleaned.

My father is taller⊙ my mother is shorter.

Australia is an island⊙ Austria is landlocked.

My grandfather is lonely⊙ we're visiting him tomorrow.

I'll sweep the kitchen⊙ you switch the laundry.

Let's charge our phones⊙ there's a storm coming.

Lesson 93

Lesson 93: Proofreading Language Arts 6

Spelling corrections are bold, punctuation marks are circled, and capitalization errors are underlined.

Have you **seen** my small striped, **collared** shirt?

M⊙ Henderson **drank two** full bottles of water.

I can't **believe** it's almost Christmas **Eve**.

Can you please **show** me **where** the bathroom is?

The teenagers came **to** the soup kitchen to **volunteer**.

Hurricane harvey **devastated** houston in 2017⊙

The **herd** of cows **was** eating grass in the **pasture**.

Whether you like it or **not**, we will be flying in a **plane**.

You **knead** the **dough** while I sprinkle in more **flour**.

"Won't you calm down?" I asked my screaming brother⊙

The dog **ate** its food so fast it almost **choked**.

I **sent** an email⊙ did you receive it?

It **pains** me to **see** you so hurt and upset⊙

The boy⊙ girl⊙ and dog went jogging to the park.

The quiz was a **surprise** to Brandy and **me**.

Lesson 94

Lesson 94: Spelling • Parts of Speech

Which choice correctly spells a word?

be_____e	sp_____e	p_____e
(liev) leev leav	erkl (arkl) ark	ree lupe (ranc)
de_____e	pe_____e	c_____e
rel (cid) lve	(rceiv) lvic nter	laf ren (raz)
k_____e	m_____e	r_____e
nowl (nif) ing	(auv) aybe arch	elive (ealiz) oinb

Use something to cover the paragraph at the bottom of the page while you fill out the blanks below according to the part of speech indicated. Then uncover the story and use your words to fill in the blanks. Was your story silly?

1. adjective: _____

2. plural noun: _____

3. ing verb: __(answers will vary)__

4. ly adverb: _____

5. adjective: _____

Don't peek until you've filled out the top section!

We took a field trip to the zoo. The _____(1)_____ _____(2)_____ were my favorite. They kept _____(3)_____ from tree to tree as _____(4)_____ as they could. It was such a _____(5)_____ day.

Lesson 95

Lesson 95: Proofreading

Spelling corrections are bold, punctuation marks are circled, and capitalization errors are underlined.

On december 16, 1773, arguably the most famous **tea** party in history took place. The british had imposed a new tax on all tea imports, and the american colonists were angry and frustrated at the amount of taxes being levied upon them. A few radical colonists **disguised** themselves as mohawk indians, took 342 crates of tea from three different british ships, and **threw** them into boston harbor. In an attempt to get even, the british shut off trade from boston until the cost of the tea should be repaid. However, **instead** of getting what they wanted, this move only served to strengthen the colonists' resolve to form a separate, independent nation. The so-called boston tea party was a big stepping stone toward the revolutionary war.

Lesson 101

Lesson 101: Proofreading

Spelling corrections are bold, punctuation marks are circled, and capitalization errors are underlined.

We went on a field trip to Mrs. Riley's farm last year. Mrs. Riley's chicken supplies **our** family with fresh eggs, so my mom thought it would be fun to see the rest of the farm. It had **rained** a lot the week before we went to the farm, and **there** was **too** much mud for my taste as a result. However, Mrs. Riley said the pigs really liked all of the mud. I don't **know** why they like it so much. One pig ran past my leg and I shouted, "ew!" as it sprayed me with mud. But Mrs. Riley had a **pair** of horses that made the **whole** day better for me. I could have watched them gallop, shake their manes, and prance about all day. Maybe I'll become a farmer someday. Of course, first they'll have to figure out a **way** to get rid of mud!

Lesson 106

Lesson 106: Spelling

Use the definitions to figure out the word that goes in the blank. Each of them start with the letter a. Alternately someone could read the words for you to spell.

To get up	a r i s e
This describes a verb	a d v e r b
Acceptance	a p p r o v a l
Period of being away	a b s e n c e
Very old	a n c i e n t
Good enough	a d e q u a t e
A lawyer	a t t o r n e y
Go up	a s c e n d
Exciting experience	a d v e n t u r e
Favorable position	a d v a n t a g e

Use these lines to complete the writing assignment from the Lesson Guide.

_____

_____

_____

_____

_____

Lesson 108

Lesson 108: Spelling
Language Arts 6

(Answers will vary. Suggestions given.)

T O L F O H D O

foot	fold
hold	loft
hood	hoot
old	foothold

O K R W B O M O

book	boom
work	room
worm	womb
bow	bookworm

K A A D R B C Y

cry	back
card	dark
drab	barky
yard	backyard

Lesson 109

Lesson 109: Participle Adjectives
Language Arts 6

Choose the correct adjective to fit the sentence.

The children were _____ by the message.
inspire (inspired) inspiring

The message was _____ to them.
inspire inspired (inspiring)

It is _____ to see their reaction.
inspire inspired (inspiring)

I am _____ by their inspiration.
inspire (inspired) inspiring

Our vacation was very _____.
relax relaxed (relaxing)

I felt very _____ on our vacation.
relax (relaxed) relaxing

Getting a massage is also _____.
relax relaxed (relaxing)

The _____ tree blocked the road.
fall (fallen) falling

Don't cry over _____ milk.
spill (spilled) spilling

Was this lesson _____ to you?
confuse confused (confusing)

Lesson 111

Lesson 111: Spelling • Writing
Language Arts 6

Use these lines to write your spelling words from the Lesson Guide. Pay attention to how they are spelled as you write them.

beautifully	calendar
disastrous	horizon
policy	vegetable
vacuum	scissors
numerator	passenger
headache	marriage
freight	capacity
arithmetic	ceiling

Lesson 112

Lesson 112: Spelling
Language Arts 6

A chart of days and weeks c a l e n d a r

Line where earth meets sky h o r i z o n

Top part of a fraction n u m e r a t o r

Contract of insurance p o l i c y

Tool used for cutting s c i s s o r s

Tool used for cleaning v a c u u m

Top of a room c e i l i n g

Maximum that can be held c a p a c i t y

Goods or cargo f r e i g h t

Math a r i t h m e t i c

Not a fruit v e g e t a b l e

A joining together m a r r i a g e

Causing great damage d i s a s t r o u s

Accompanies a driver p a s s e n g e r

Pain in the head h e a d a c h e

Lesson 114

Find your spelling words along with some extras in the word search below. Words can be found in any direction.

beautifully	calendar	disastrous	horizon
numerator	passenger	policy	vegetable
vacuum	scissors	headache	marriage
capacity	arithmetic	ceiling	freight

Lesson 115

See how many words you can spell correctly now that you've had a few chances to practice. Have someone read them to you.

arithmetic	beautifully
calendar	capacity
ceiling	disastrous
freight	headache
horizon	marriage
numerator	passenger
policy	scissors
vacuum	vegetable

Lesson 116

Can you spell even more words correctly this time? Have someone read them to you. Learn from any mistakes you make.

headache	horizon
scissors	numerator
freight	disastrous
ceiling	arithmetic
beautifully	vacuum
capacity	vegetable
policy	calendar
marriage	passenger

Lesson 117

Use these lines to write your spelling words from the Lesson Guide. Pay attention to how they are spelled as you write them.

chrome	zealous
oxygen	laughter
interested	opposite
decrease	imply
foliage	beguiled
difficulty	archaeologist
cantaloupe	parliament
sensitive	jealousy

Lesson 118

Lesson 118: Spelling

Find your spelling words in the word search below. Words are in every direction.

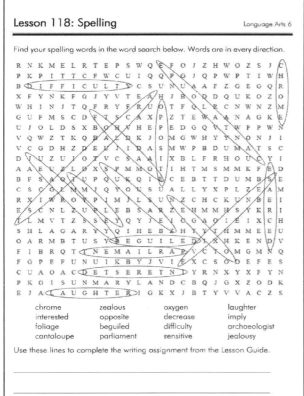

chrome   zealous   oxygen   laughter
interested   opposite   decrease   imply
foliage   beguiled   difficulty   archaeologist
cantaloupe   parliament   sensitive   jealousy

Use these lines to complete the writing assignment from the Lesson Guide.

Lesson 119

Lesson 119: Spelling • Grammar

Unscramble the letters below into the correctly spelled word they represent.

EGBEDULI
__beguiled__

YFICLIDFUT
__difficulty__

OGLFIEA
__foliage__

VESITNIES
__sensitive__

PCNEATAOLU
__cantaloupe__

MALNAPERTI
__parliament__

Of the bolded words, circle the one that matches the part of speech to the side of the sentence. Then use the lines for your writing assignment.

Somewhere (over) the rainbow, bluebirds fly.   Preposition

The (painting) was displayed above the tub.   Noun

Her (lovely) eyes sparkled under her glasses.   Adjective

Pick up your shoes and put (them) in the bin.   Pronoun

The (normally) lively dog was acting mellow.   Adverb

Your mom (will) decide what to fix for dinner.   Verb

Lesson 120-1

Lesson 120: Spelling • Participles

Have someone read you your spelling words as you write them below. Hopefully they're getting easier to spell as you work with them more.

archaeologist	beguiled
cantaloupe	chrome
decrease	difficulty
foliage	imply
interested	jealousy
opposite	oxygen
laughter	parliament
sensitive	zealous

(continued on next page)

Lesson 120-2

Lesson 120: Spelling • Participles

In these sentences, underline the participles and circle the words they modify.

His frown was evidence of his broken (spirit.)

My sister captivates everyone with her smiling (eyes.)

The injured (bunny) fully recovered.

I was awakened early by the singing (bird.)

In these sentences, underline the participial phrases and circle the words they modify.

Refreshed from her nap, (Sarah) ran wild.

The (shopkeeper,) having sold all of his goods, closed his store.

Smiling nervously, (Lucas) sang his solo.

The (children,) having been warned, didn't venture out of the yard.

In these sentences, underline the infinitive phrases and circle the words they modify.

Pizza is the best (meal) to eat.

Jason is the (one) to ask about photography.

If you'll excuse me, I have a (plane) to catch.

Your (suggestion) to read this book was fantastic.

Lesson 121

Lesson 121: Adjectives and Adverbs
Language Arts 6

Can you change the listed adjectives into their adverb forms? For instance: The dog was *quick*. He ran *quickly*. If you get stuck, try plugging the words into that sentence and see if you can figure it out. Most of them are easy, but there are a few tricky ones! Use the lines at the bottom for your writing assignment.

jealous	anxious
jealously	**anxiously**
angry	curious
angrily	**curiously**
bold	zealous
boldly	**zealously**
sad	good
sadly	**well**
fast	generous
fast	**generously**
happy	responsible
happily	**responsibly**
hot	hurtful
hotly	**hurtfully**

Lesson 125-1

Lesson 125: English Review
Language Arts 6

Answer the questions below to see how well you remember some of the things we've learned during this course.

Which of these is an example of a participle adjective?
- ○ snowy
- ○ extra-cold snow
- ● fallen snow

Bear and bare are examples of...
- ● homonyms
- ○ antonyms
- ○ synonyms

Which is a compound sentence?
- ○ Since I didn't go to bed on time, I'm really tired.
- ● I need to go to bed, or I'll be really tired tomorrow.
- ○ I need to go to bed now!

When I get up in the morning is a (an)...
- ● dependent clause
- ○ independent clause

Which is a complex sentence?
- ○ I need to get on my pjs, brush my teeth, say goodnight, and get into bed.
- ○ I need to go to bed, or I'll be really tired tomorrow.
- ● When I get up in the morning, I'm going to be really tired.

"The snow was a blanket on the lawn" is an example of...
- ○ alliteration
- ● a metaphor
- ○ a simile

"The skaters darted out like water bugs" is an example of...
- ○ alliteration
- ○ a metaphor
- ● a simile

(continued on next page)

Lesson 125-2

Lesson 125: English Review
Language Arts 6

How many pronouns are in this sentence? They think they can do it all themselves.
- ○ 5
- ● 4
- ○ 3

Which of these words has a prefix?
- ● unprepared
- ○ notorious
- ○ creative

Where should the main idea or thesis be stated in an essay's introductory paragraph?
- ○ in every sentence
- ● in the last sentence
- ○ in the first sentence

Which of these is correct?
- ○ "I need you now!" He said.
- ● "I need you now!" he said.
- ○ "I need you now." he said.

Which word in this sentence is an adverb? It was rather hot when I went in for the early show.
- ○ early
- ● rather
- ○ in

A compound sentence is made up of...
- ● two independent clauses
- ○ two dependent clauses
- ○ an independent clause and a dependent clause

I would like eggs for breakfast is an example of a (an)...
- ○ dependent clause
- ● independent clause

Lesson 141

Lesson 141: Common Verb Mistakes
Language Arts 6

These verbs are commonly misused. Try to match the verb with its definition. Learn from any mistakes you make.

rise	C	A. past tense of lay
raised	H	B. past tense of lie
have raised	F	C. to get up
rose	J	D. rest in an upright position
lie	G	E. past tense of sit
lay	B	F. past participle of raise
laid	A	G. rest in a reclining position
set	I	H. past tense of raise
sat	E	I. put or place something
sit	D	J. past tense of rise

See if you can figure out the right time to use lay and the right time to use lie.

My dog is _____ by the door.	He often _____ here.
○ laying ● lying	○ lays ● lies
He has _____ here many times.	He _____ here just this morning.
○ laid ● lain	○ laid ● lay
Birds _____ eggs.	A hen _____ over 200 eggs a year.
● lay ○ lie	● lays ○ lies
I _____ my toothbrush on the sink.	The US _____ to the south of Canada.
○ lay ● laid	● lies ○ lays

Lesson 142

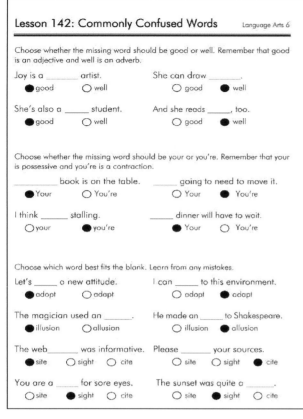

Lesson 142: Commonly Confused Words Language Arts 6

Choose whether the missing word should be good or well. Remember that good is an adjective and well is an adverb.

Joy is a _____ artist.
● good   ○ well

She can draw _____.
○ good   ● well

She's also a _____ student.
● good   ○ well

And she reads _____, too.
○ good   ● well

Choose whether the missing word should be your or you're. Remember that your is possessive and you're is a contraction.

_____ book is on the table.
● Your   ○ You're

_____ going to need to move it.
○ Your   ● You're

I think _____ stalling.
○ your   ● you're

_____ dinner will have to wait.
● Your   ○ You're

Choose which word best fits the blank. Learn from any mistakes.

Let's _____ a new attitude.
● adopt   ○ adapt

I can _____ to this environment.
○ adopt   ● adapt

The magician used an _____.
● illusion   ○ allusion

He made an _____ to Shakespeare.
○ illusion   ● allusion

The web_____ was informative.
● site   ○ sight   ○ cite

Please _____ your sources.
○ site   ○ sight   ● cite

You are a _____ for sore eyes.
○ site   ● sight   ○ cite

The sunset was quite a _____.
○ site   ● sight   ○ cite

Lesson 143

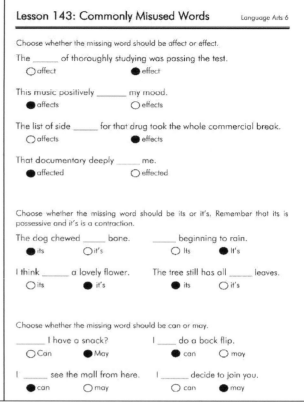

Lesson 143: Commonly Misused Words Language Arts 6

Choose whether the missing word should be affect or effect.

The _____ of thoroughly studying was passing the test.
○ affect   ● effect

This music positively _____ my mood.
● affects   ○ effects

The list of side _____ for that drug took the whole commercial break.
○ affects   ● effects

That documentary deeply _____ me.
● affected   ○ effected

Choose whether the missing word should be its or it's. Remember that its is possessive and it's is a contraction.

The dog chewed _____ bone.
● its   ○ it's

_____ beginning to rain.
○ Its   ● It's

I think _____ a lovely flower.
○ its   ● it's

The tree still has all _____ leaves.
● its   ○ it's

Choose whether the missing word should be can or may.

_____ I have a snack?
○ Can   ● May

I _____ do a back flip.
● can   ○ may

I _____ see the mall from here.
● can   ○ may

I _____ decide to join you.
○ can   ● may

Lesson 144

Lesson 144: Dependent Clauses Language Arts 6

Choose which part of the following sentences is the dependent clause.

When we left home yesterday, I forgot to bring my toothbrush.
● when we left home yesterday
○ I forgot to bring my toothbrush

Maybe we can find a store when we get to our destination.
○ maybe we can find a store
● when we get to our destination

If I don't get a chance to brush them, my teeth start to feel fuzzy.
● if I don't get a chance to brush them
○ my teeth start to feel fuzzy

If I can't get a toothbrush, I'll have to find some minty gum.
● if I can't get a toothbrush
○ I'll have to find some minty gum

(Answers will vary. Suggestions given.)

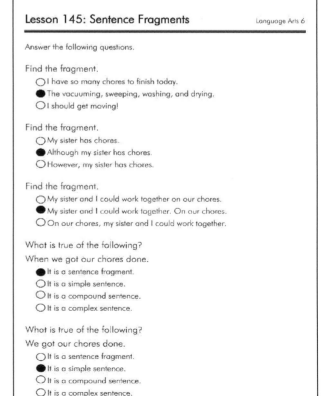

Freemont, the busiest street in town, cuts right through the downtown area.

The leaves, falling off the trees, temporarily obstruct my view when I'm driving.

Lesson 145

Lesson 145: Sentence Fragments Language Arts 6

Answer the following questions.

Find the fragment.
○ I have so many chores to finish today.
● The vacuuming, sweeping, washing, and drying.
○ I should get moving!

Find the fragment.
○ My sister has chores.
● Although my sister has chores.
○ However, my sister has chores.

Find the fragment.
○ My sister and I could work together on our chores.
● My sister and I could work together. On our chores.
○ On our chores, my sister and I could work together.

What is true of the following?
When we got our chores done.
● It is a sentence fragment.
○ It is a simple sentence.
○ It is a compound sentence.
○ It is a complex sentence.

What is true of the following?
We got our chores done.
○ It is a sentence fragment.
● It is a simple sentence.
○ It is a compound sentence.
○ It is a complex sentence.

Lesson 146

Underline the part of each paragraph that is a fragment.

I went for a jog yesterday afternoon. As I turned the corner, I stumbled face first into a large mud puddle. I stood up and looked around, completely embarrassed. As mud and water dripped down my face and clothes. I decided jogging wasn't for me.

Sylvia went to the mall food court for lunch with her friends. The vast choices overwhelmed her. Japanese, Chinese, subs, pizza, chicken, burgers and fries. It took her longer to decide what she wanted to eat than it did to finish her meal.

Clothes shopping was not fun for Peter. He just didn't care what he wore, as long as he was dressed. Some of his friends were more particular. For instance, Christopher's plaid shirts or Logan's stripes. Peter wasn't particular enough to enjoy shopping for clothes.

Beth was helping her mom with some baking. It smelled like something was burning. Beth opened the oven. Which caused her glasses to fog up with steam. Her mom chuckled and scooped up the fallen, burning chocolate chip and dumped it in the trash.

Lesson 147

Choose a piece from each box to build a word that fits the blank in the sentence.

dis	cal
hor	bea
jeal	sep
sen	not

i	ous
ara	ice
si	en
utif	as

tely	able
tive	y
trous	ully
dar	zon

The tear in your skirt is hardly ___noticeable___.

I could sense her ___jealousy___ as I described my new, adorable puppy.

The sun is setting beyond the ___horizon___.

My eyes are so ___sensitive___ to light that I need prescription sunglasses.

The missing screw had ___disastrous___ consequences.

I forgot to turn the ___calendar___ to the new month, so my days are all off.

The song was ___beautifully___ performed.

I think we should drive ___separately___ so we have two cars there.

Lesson 148

Underline the part of each paragraph that is a fragment.

It takes forever to get ready for bed. For some reason, I'm so distractible while I'm trying to do everything. Brushing my teeth, changing my clothes, washing my face, saying my prayers. It's easy to let my mind wander and slow me down.

My favorite game is one where you get to be the mayor of your own city. But it's not all sunshine and roses. You have to make sure there are pipes running water to the city. And lines running electricity. When things aren't going well, your whole city is mad at you. But when things are great, they sing your praises.

On the way to musical rehearsal, we got a flat tire. We have roadside assistance, but they said it would be an hour before they could come. We opted to walk. It was a beautiful day. Good thing!

Jessica's bedroom is a mess. Piles of dirty clothes, clean clothes, dirty dishes, and toys. The crazy thing is that it was just cleaned yesterday. She'll have to clean it again tomorrow. It's bedtime now.

Lesson 152

For each blank in the sentences below, fill in a comma if a comma belongs. Fill in an x if a comma doesn't belong.

Charise wants to be a librarian _x_ when she grows up_,_ so in addition to studying literature _x_ and reading as much as she can _,_ she also helps sort_,_ stack_,_ and put away the books _x_ at her local library.

"Hey Brian_,_" _x_ I called to my brother._x_ "Do you know where we left the football _x_ when we were done playing with it last week?" Brian answered _x_ that he couldn't remember where he had put it.

On the way _x_ to the store _,_ my mom saw an albino deer running through the trees _,_ so she opted to skip the store _x_ to attempt to get its picture.

One dark _,_ stormy night _,_ my sisters and I were huddled in the basement. Suddenly _,_ our brothers jumped out from behind the couch _,_ startling us all.

Having read and loved all of the author's books _,_ I was greatly looking forward to her book release _x_ the following day. 4

Lesson 153

Fill in the missing punctuation in the sentences below.

"What was your answer," asked Tricia, "about going dinner tonight?"

When we drove through Texas, we visited the following cities: El Paso, San Antonio, and Houston.

The cute-as-a-button baby made cooing noises.

Before you leave for the store, make sure that you have the grocery list.

"I think," stuttered Jen, "that I need to take a break."

Fill in any missing apostrophes in the sentences below.

Sarah, Jenny, and Lisa all made the girls' soccer team.

Sarah and Jenny remembered their shin guards, but Lisa's were left at home.

Without shin guards, she couldn't take part in the scrimmage at practice.

She didn't forget them on game day, though!

She brought hers and a spare for anyone else who might have forgotten theirs. **(none needed)**

Lesson 154

Of the bolded words, underline the one that matches the part of speech to the side of the sentence.

It's a special treat to get to eat **in** my bed.   Preposition

Let's go for a **run** first thing in the morning.   Noun

That was such a **relaxing** vacation to Maui.   Adjective

We are headed to the park after lunch.   Pronoun

The **Very** Hungry Caterpillar is a great book.   Adverb

The dance at the Rec Center **was** a lot of fun.   Verb

Circle the part of speech that correctly labels the underlined word in each sentence.

It's pouring down rain outside!   **(noun)** adverb adjective

Did you ask them to join us?   noun **(pronoun)** adverb

Look at that deer over there!   verb **(preposition)** noun

The fascinating story captivated me.   noun verb **(adjective)**

We had a great trip to the fair.   adverb **(verb)** preposition

Will you be here soon?   noun **(adverb)** pronoun

Lesson 163

Each sentence contains an appositive. Select the correctly punctuated option from the list of choices.

The scariest animal I've ever seen was in our yard a rabid coyote.
- ○ The scariest animal I've ever seen, was in our yard, a rabid coyote.
- ● The scariest animal I've ever seen was in our yard, a rabid coyote.
- ○ The scariest animal, I've ever seen, was in our yard a rabid coyote.

My birthday a week from Thursday will be a busy day.
- ● My birthday, a week from Thursday, will be a busy day.
- ○ My birthday, a week from Thursday will be, a busy day.
- ○ My birthday, a week from Thursday will be a busy day.

The star of the show Julie Andrews has a beautiful voice.
- ○ The star of the show Julie Andrews, has a beautiful voice.
- ○ The star, of the show, Julie Andrews has a beautiful voice.
- ● The star of the show, Julie Andrews, has a beautiful voice.

Jason is our best quarterback the boy wearing number 12.
- ● Jason is our best quarterback, the boy wearing number 12.
- ○ Jason, is our best quarterback, the boy wearing number 12.
- ○ Jason is our best quarterback the boy, wearing number 12.

My favorite activities singing and dancing have a time and a place.
- ○ My favorite activities singing and dancing have a time, and a place.
- ○ My favorite activities singing, and dancing have a time, and a place.
- ● My favorite activities, singing and dancing, have a time and a place.

My friend Angie likes to read.
- ○ My friend, Angie likes to read.
- ● My friend Angie likes to read.
- ○ My friend, Angie, likes to read.

Lesson 164

Fill in the past tense form of the verb given in parentheses.

(wind) If you ___**wound**___ your watch, why did it stop?

(drive) We ___**drove**___ to Sacramento in one night.

(kneel) My dad ___**knelt**___ beside me as I prayed.

(ring) The phone ___**rang**___ four times before stopping.

(grow) The little seed ___**grew**___ into a huge bush.

Identify the appositives in the following sentences.

My sister Emily has a lot of shoes.
- ○ My
- ○ Sister
- ● Emily
- ○ Shoes

The word "shoes" makes me think of blisters and trapped toes.
- ○ The word
- ● shoes
- ○ makes
- ○ trapped

I, the queen of comfort, would be barefoot all the time if I could be.
- ○ I
- ● the queen of comfort
- ○ all the time
- ○ if I could be

Lesson 165

The threat of impending storms causes me undue stress.

At face value, your idea seems to have merit.

I asked you to pick up milk, not eggs.

Bring your pennies, nickels, and dimes to the fundraiser tomorrow.

My cousin, a soccer player, likes to run for fun.

(Answers will vary. Suggestions given.)

My grandparents live in a simple farm house on Shadowfax Drive in Gentryville, where they are neighbors of the mayor.

Their yard has a large apple tree whose branches hold a fantastic swing from which we jump into the creek behind the tree.

We hope you had a great year with EP Language Arts 6.

EP provides free, complete, high quality online homeschool curriculum for children around the world. Find more of our courses and resources on our site, allinonehomeschool.com.

_____

If you prefer offline materials, consider Genesis Curriculum which takes a book of the Bible and turns it into daily lessons in science, social studies, and language arts for your children to learn all together. The curriculum also includes learning Biblical languages. Genesis Curriculum offers Rainbow Readers and A Mind for Math, a math curriculum designed for about first through fourth grade to be done all together. Each math lesson is based on the day's Bible reading from the main curriculum. GC Steps is an offline preschool and kindergarten program. Learn more about our curriculum on our site, GenesisCurriculum.com.

Made in the USA
Las Vegas, NV
07 December 2020